From Data to Decisions:

Business Analytics with R

by Jeff Monroe

Table of Content

Prologue

In the bustling world of data-driven decision-making, businesses strive to harness the power of information to gain a competitive edge, "From Data to Decisions: Business Analytics with R" is a guiding light for those embarking on mastering R programming and business analytics. This book is crafted with a specific audience in mind, aiming to cater to the needs of aspiring data analysts, business professionals, and students eager to dive into data science.

Aspiring Data Analysts: If you are a budding data analyst eager to uncover insights from vast amounts of data, this book is your ideal companion. Whether you are just starting your journey or looking to solidify your understanding of R programming, "From Data to Decisions: Business Analytics with R" offers a structured and practical approach to learning. Through hands-on tutorials and real-world examples, you will build a strong foundation in data manipulation, visualization, and statistical analysis, setting you up for a successful career in data analytics.

Business Professionals: For business professionals aiming to make data-driven decisions, this book provides the tools and knowledge to translate complex data into actionable insights. If you are a manager, consultant, or executive looking to enhance your analytical skills, "From Data to Decisions: Business Analytics with R" will equip you with the ability to leverage R programming to analyze financial data, understand customer behavior, forecast sales, and optimize operational processes. The practical examples and case studies will resonate with real-world challenges, helping you apply analytical techniques directly to your business context.

Students and Academics: This book is an invaluable resource for students pursuing degrees in business, economics, computer science, or related fields. The structured learning path, from basic R commands to advanced analytics techniques, aligns well with academic curricula, providing a comprehensive supplement to classroom learning. Academics and educators can also use this book as a reference or textbook, guiding their students through the practical applications of business analytics using R.

Self-Learners and Enthusiasts: If you are a self-learner passionate about data science and eager to expand your skill set, "From Data to Decisions: Business Analytics with R" offers a detailed and engaging approach to mastering R programming. The book's narrative, following Alex's journey at BizTech Solutions, makes learning enjoyable and relatable, encouraging you to immerse yourself in data analytics at your own pace.

"From Data to Decisions: Business Analytics with R" is designed to demystify the complexities of R programming and business analytics, making them accessible to a diverse audience. Whether stepping into the world of data for the first time or seeking to refine your existing skills, this book will guide you through data analysis, empowering you to make informed decisions and drive success in your professional endeavors. Join us on this enlightening journey, and let "From Data to Decisions: Business Analytics with R" be your roadmap to mastering the art of business analytics.

Code and datasets used throughout this book may be found on GitHub:

https://github.com/jtmonroe252/Data-to-Decisions

Joining BizTech Solutions

Chapter 1: Welcome to BizTech Solutions

The early morning sun cast a warm glow over the bustling city as Alex stood in front of BizTech Solutions' towering glass building. The buzz of commuters and the hum of the city's life surrounded him, but his mind was focused on the journey ahead. Clutching his briefcase, he took a deep breath and stepped through the revolving doors into the grand lobby, where the company's slogan, "Innovate. Analyze. Transform," greeted him in bold letters.

Alex had always been passionate about data and its potential to solve real-world problems. After years of studying and refining his skills in R programming, he finally secured a position as a business analyst at BizTech Solutions, a leading firm renowned for its innovative approach to business analytics. Today he marked the beginning of his journey to apply his knowledge in a dynamic, real-world environment.

"Welcome to BizTech Solutions, Alex," greeted Jenna, the HR manager, with a warm smile as she approached him in the lobby. "We're excited to have you on board. Let me show you around and introduce you to your new team."

Jenna led Alex through the sleek, modern corridors of the building, highlighting the various departments and their roles. The Finance department, with its sharp focus on financial analysis and forecasting; the vibrant Marketing department, where creativity met data to drive customer engagement; the Sales department, always buzzing with activity and competitive energy; and finally, the Operations department, the backbone that ensured everything ran smoothly.

As they walked, Jenna shared stories of successful projects and the collaborative culture at BizTech. Alex listened intently, eager to absorb every detail. They finally reached his new home – the Finance department.

"This is Lisa, the head of our Finance team," Jenna introduced him to a poised woman with a keen eye for detail. "She'll be your mentor for the next few weeks."

"Welcome, Alex," Lisa said, shaking his hand. "We've got a lot of exciting work ahead. Let's get you settled and dive right in."

Technical Tutorial: Introduction to R and its Importance in Business Analytics

Overview: This section will cover the basics of R, a powerful programming language used for statistical computing and graphics. R is widely used in business analytics due to its versatility and the extensive range of packages available for data analysis, visualization, and machine learning.

Getting Started with R:

1. Installing R and RStudio:

- Download and install R from CRAN.
- Download and install RStudio, an integrated development environment (IDE) for R, from RStudio.

2. Setting Up RStudio:

- Open RStudio and familiarize yourself with the interface, including the Console, Script Editor, Environment, and Plots panes.

3. Basic R Commands:

- Let's start with some basic R commands to get comfortable with the syntax.

```
# Basic arithmetic operations
2 + 2
5 - 3
4 * 3
8 / 2

# Assigning values to variables
x <- 10
y <- 5

# Basic operations with variables
sum <- x + y
difference <- x - y
product <- x * y
quotient <- x / y

# Print values
print(sum)
15
print(difference)
5
print(product)
50
print(quotient)
2
```

Data Structures in R:

- Learn about different data structures in R, such as vectors, matrices, data frames, and lists.

Vectors:

```
# Create a numeric vector
numbers <- c(1, 2, 3, 4, 5)
print(numbers)
1 2 3 4 5
```

```r
# Perform operations on vectors
sum_numbers <- sum(numbers)
mean_numbers <- mean(numbers)

print(sum_numbers)
15
print(mean_numbers)
        3
```

Data Frames:

```r
# Create a data frame
data <- data.frame(
  Name = c("John", "Jane", "Alex", "Emily"),
  Age = c(28, 24, 30, 22),
  Department = c("Finance", "Marketing", "Sales",
"Operations")
)
print(data)
```

Name	Age	Department
John	28	Finance
Jane	24	Marketing
Alex	30	Sales
Emily	22	Operations

```r
# Access data frame columns
print(data$Name)
```

```
    "John" "Jane" "Alex" "Emily"
```

```r
print(data$Age)
28 24 30 22
```

```r
# Summary statistics
summary(data)
```

Name	Age	Department
Length:4	Min. :22.0	Length:4
Class :character	1st Qu.:23.5	Class :character
Mode :character	Median :26.0	Mode :character
	Mean :26.0	
	3rd Qu.:28.5	
	Max. :30.0	

Using Packages:

- R's functionality can be significantly extended with packages. Let's install and load a popular package for data manipulation.

  ```
  # Install the dplyr package
  install.packages("dplyr")

  # Load the dplyr package
  library(dplyr)

  # Use dplyr to manipulate data
  data_filtered <- filter(data, Age > 25)

  print(data_filtered)
  ```

Name	Age	Department
John	28	Finance
Alex	30	Sales

Exercises:

1. Installing R and RStudio:

   - Ensure you have R and RStudio installed on your computer.
   - Open RStudio and familiarize yourself with the interface.

2. Basic R Commands:

   - Write a script to perform basic arithmetic operations.
   - Assign values to variables and perform operations on them.

3. Data Structures:

   - Create a numeric vector and calculate its sum and mean.
   - Create a data frame with sample data and perform basic operations on it.

4. Using Packages:

   - Install and load the dplyr package.
   - Use dplyr to filter and manipulate a data frame.

By the end of this chapter, you should have a solid understanding of R's basics and be ready to dive into more complex business analytics tasks. Alex's journey at BizTech Solutions is just beginning, and so is your adventure with R programming.

Chapter 2: Common Errors and Troubleshooting

In any programming journey, encountering errors is inevitable. Understanding and troubleshooting these errors is a crucial skill that will help you become a more proficient programmer. This chapter will cover some common errors you might encounter while working with R, along with tips on how to troubleshoot and resolve them.

1. Syntax Errors

Error Description: Syntax errors occur when the code you write does not follow the rules of the R language.

Common Examples:

- Missing parentheses, braces, or commas.
- Misspelled function names.

Troubleshooting Tips:

- Read the Error Message: R's error messages often indicate where the syntax error occurred. Look for line numbers and error descriptions.
- Check Punctuation: Ensure that all parentheses, braces, and

commas are correctly placed.
- Use a Code Editor: Use an integrated development environment (IDE) like RStudio, which highlights syntax errors as you type.

Example:

```
# Incorrect
print("Hello, World!"

# Correct
print("Hello, World!")

    "Hello, World!"
```

2. Object Not Found

Error Description: This error occurs when you try to use a variable or function that has not been defined.

Common Examples:

- Using a variable before it has been assigned a value.
- Misspelling a variable or function name.

Troubleshooting Tips:

- Check Variable Names: Ensure that the variable or function name is spelled correctly and that it has been defined.
- Use ls(): Use the ls() function to list all objects in the current environment to check if the object exists.

Example:

```
# Incorrect
print(x)
```

```
# Correct
x <- 10
print(x)
        10
```

3. Data Type Errors

Error Description: These errors occur when the data type of an object is not what the function expects.

Common Examples:

- Passing a character string to a function that expects a numeric value.
- Trying to perform arithmetic operations on non-numeric data.

Troubleshooting Tips:

- Check Data Types: Use the class() or typeof() functions to check the data type of an object.
- Convert Data Types: Use functions like as.numeric(), as.character(), etc., to convert data types as needed.

Example:

```
# Incorrect
x <- "10"
sum(x)

# Correct
x <- as.numeric("10")
sum(x)
        10
```

4. Package Not Found

Error Description: This error occurs when you try to use a package that has not been installed or loaded.

Common Examples:

- Forgetting to install a package.
- Forgetting to load a package with the library() function.

Troubleshooting Tips:

- Install the Package: Use install.packages("package_name") to install the package.
- Load the Package: Use library(package_name) to load the package into the current session.

Example:

```
# Incorrect
library(ggplot2)
ggplot(mtcars, aes(x = mpg, y = wt)) + geom_point()

# Correct
install.packages("ggplot2")
library(ggplot2)
ggplot(mtcars, aes(x = mpg, y = wt)) + geom_point()
```

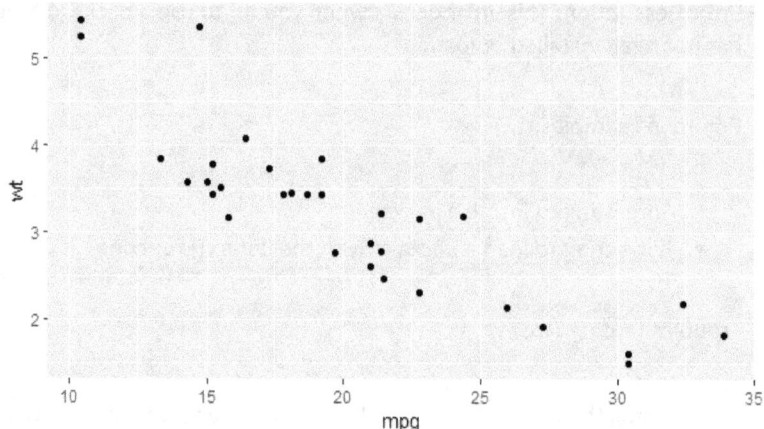

5. Function Argument Errors

Error Description: These errors occur when the arguments passed to a function are incorrect or missing.

Common Examples:

- Missing required arguments.
- Passing arguments in the wrong order.
- Using incorrect argument names.

Troubleshooting Tips:

- Check Function Documentation: Use ?function_name to view the documentation for the function and ensure you are using the correct arguments.
- Provide Named Arguments: Use named arguments to avoid confusion about the order of arguments.

Example:

```
# Incorrect
```

plot(mtcars$mpg, main = "MPG vs. Weight")

Correct
plot(mtcars$mpg, mtcars$wt, main = "MPG vs. Weight")

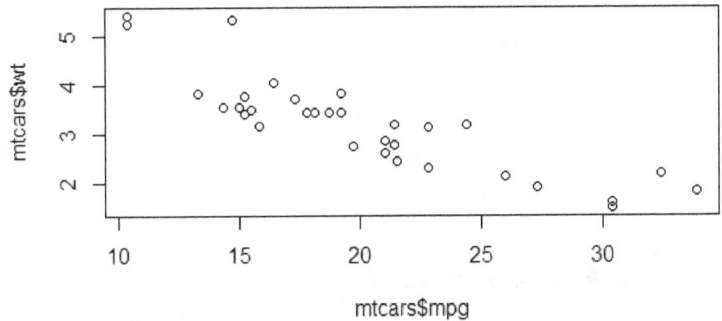

MPG vs. Weight

6. Index Out of Bounds

Error Description: This error occurs when you try to access an element of a vector, list, or data frame that does not exist.

Common Examples:

- Using an index that is larger than the length of the vector.
- Using a negative or zero index.

Troubleshooting Tips:

- Check Index Values: Ensure that the index values are within the valid range.
- Use length(): Use the length() function to check the length of the object before indexing.

Example:

```
# Incorrect
x <- c(1, 2, 3)
x[4]

# Correct
x <- c(1, 2, 3)
if (length(x) >= 4) {
  print(x[4])
} else {
  print("Index out of bounds")
}
```

"Index out of bounds"

7. Memory Allocation Errors

Error Description: These errors occur when R runs out of memory while trying to perform an operation.

Common Examples:

- Working with very large datasets.
- Performing memory-intensive operations.

Troubleshooting Tips:

- Increase Memory Limit: On Windows, use memory.limit(size = X) to increase the memory limit.
- Use Efficient Data Structures: Use data.table instead of data.frame for large datasets.
- Clean Up Memory: Use rm() to remove unnecessary objects and gc() to perform garbage collection.

Example:

```
# Clean up memory
rm(list = ls())
gc()
```

Conclusion

Encountering errors is a natural part of the learning process in programming. By understanding common errors and learning how to troubleshoot them, you will become a more confident and capable R programmer. Keep practicing, and don't be discouraged by mistakes— each error is an opportunity to learn and improve.

By following these tips and utilizing the troubleshooting techniques covered in this chapter, you'll be well-equipped to handle the challenges you encounter in your journey through data analysis with R.

Chapter 3: Data Cleaning

Alex stood at his new desk at BizTech Solutions, feeling a mix of excitement and determination. Lisa, his mentor, had just given him an important task: to clean and prepare a new dataset for an upcoming analysis project.

"Data cleaning is a critical step in any data analysis process, Alex," Lisa explained. "Ensuring the data is accurate and consistent will make our analysis much more reliable. Today, you'll learn how to handle missing values, remove duplicates, correct inconsistencies, and prepare the data for further analysis."

With a nod, Alex opened his laptop and got to work. He knew that mastering data cleaning would be an essential skill in his journey as a data analyst.

Introduction

Data cleaning involves identifying and correcting (or removing) errors and inconsistencies in data to improve its quality. This process includes handling missing values, removing duplicates, correcting inconsistencies, and ensuring data is in a proper format for analysis.

By the end of this chapter, you will be able to:

1. Identify and handle missing values.

2. Remove duplicate entries.
3. Correct data inconsistencies.
4. Format and normalize data.
5. Validate and verify data accuracy.

Loading Data

First, let's load a sample dataset to work with. For this chapter, we will use a dataset called customer_data.csv, which contains information about customers, including their names, ages, purchase history, and more.

Alex loaded the dataset into R and examined the first few rows to get a sense of what he was working with.

```
# Load necessary libraries
install.packages("tidyverse")
library(tidyverse)

# Load the dataset
customer_data <-
read.csv("https://raw.githubusercontent.com/jtmonroe252/D
ata-to-Decisions/main/data/customer_data.csv")

# View the first few rows of the dataset
head(customer_data)
```

Customer_ID	Name	Age	Gender	Purchase_Amount	Registration_Date
Min. : 1.00	Length:70	Min. :18.00	Length:70	Min. : 250.8	Length:70
1st Qu.:17.25	Class :character	1st Qu.:28.00	Class :character	1st Qu.: 597.5	Class :character
Median :34.50	Mode :character	Median :40.00	Mode :character	Median : 718.0	Mode :character
Mean :34.23		Mean :39.39		Mean : 742.3	
3rd Qu.:50.75		3rd Qu.:50.00		3rd Qu.: 902.5	
Max. :68.00		Max. :55.00		Max. :1266.5	

Handling Missing Values

Missing values are common in real-world datasets and can arise from various reasons such as data entry errors or unrecorded information. R provides several ways to handle missing values.

Identifying Missing Values

First, let's identify where the missing values are in our dataset. Alex knew this step was crucial to understand the extent of the problem.

```
# Check for missing values
summary(customer_data)

# Visualize missing data
install.packages("naniar")
library(naniar)
Vis_miss(customer_data)
```

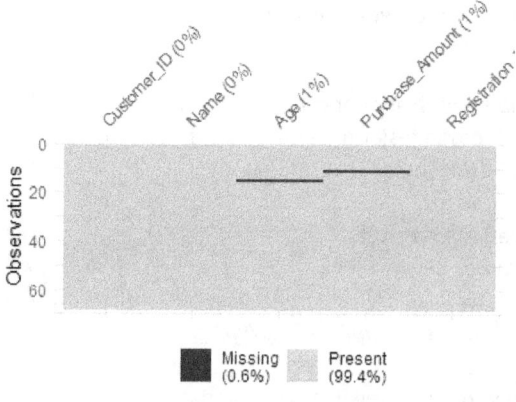

Removing Missing Values

One approach to handle missing values is to remove any rows containing them.

```
# Remove rows with any missing values
cleaned_data <- na.omit(customer_data)

# Verify the changes
summary(cleaned_data)
```

Customer_ID	Name	Age	Gender	Purchase_Amount	Registration_Date
Min. : 1.00	Length:69	Min. :18.00	Length:69	Min. : 250.8	Length:69
1st Qu.:18.00	Class :character	1st Qu.:28.00	Class :character	1st Qu.: 595.4	Class :character
Median :35.00	Mode :character	Median :40.00	Mode :character	Median : 715.7	Mode :character
Mean :34.51		Mean :39.39		Mean : 739.6	
3rd Qu.:51.00		3rd Qu.:50.00		3rd Qu.: 897.3	
Max. :68.00		Max. :55.00		Max. :1266.5	

Imputing Missing Values

In some cases, it might be better to replace missing values with a meaningful substitute rather than removing the entire row. Common strategies include using the mean, median, or mode of the column.

```
# Impute missing values with the mean for numeric columns
customer_data$Age[is.na(customer_data$Age)] <-
mean(customer_data$Age, na.rm = TRUE)
customer_data$Purchase_Amount[is.na(customer_data$Purc
hase_Amount)] <- mean(customer_data$Purchase_Amount,
na.rm = TRUE)

# Verify the changes
summary(customer_data)
```

Customer_ID	Name	Age	Gender	Purchase_Amount	Registration_Date
1	John Doe	36	Male	650.75	6/15/2021
2	Jane Smith	22	Female	661.25	12/22/2020
3	Alex Johnson	47	Male	958.86	2/9/2021
4	Emily Davis	23	Female	666.2	7/3/2021
5	Chris White	55	Male	506.21	1/18/2021
6	Sam Brown	40	Male	822.74	5/25/2021

Removing Duplicates

Duplicate entries can skew your analysis results. It's important to identify and remove duplicates.

Alex scanned the dataset for duplicate entries, a task that required careful attention to detail.

```
# Check for duplicate rows
duplicates <- customer_data[duplicated(customer_data),]
```

```
# Remove duplicate rows
customer_data <-
customer_data[!duplicated(customer_data),]

# Verify the changes
summary(customer_data)
```

Customer_ID	Name	Age	Gender	Purchase_Amount	Registration_Date
Min. : 1.00	Length:68	Min. :18.00	Length:68	Min. : 250.8	Length:68
1st Qu.:17.75	Class :character	1st Qu.:27.75	Class :character	1st Qu.: 591.5	Class :character
Median :34.50	Mode :character	Median :40.00	Mode :character	Median : 718.0	Mode :character
Mean :34.50		Mean :38.95		Mean : 739.8	
3rd Qu.:51.25		3rd Qu.:49.00		3rd Qu.: 899.1	
Max. :68.00		Max. :55.00		Max. :1266.5	

Correcting Inconsistencies

Data inconsistencies can arise from different formats, typographical errors, or varying representations of the same information. It's crucial to standardize these entries.

```
# Convert all names to title case
customer_data$Name <- str_to_title(customer_data$Name)

# Correct typos or inconsistencies in categorical data
customer_data$Gender <- ifelse(customer_data$Gender ==
"M", "Male",                ifelse(customer_data$Gender
== "F", "Female", customer_data$Gender))

# Verify the changes
head(customer_data)
```

Customer_ID	Name	Age	Gender	Purchase_Amount	Registration_Date
1	John Doe	36	Male	650.75	6/15/2021
2	Jane Smit	22	Female	661.25	12/22/2020
3	Alex John	47	Male	958.86	2/9/2021
4	Emily Dav	23	Female	666.2	7/3/2021
5	Chris Whi	55	Male	506.21	1/18/2021
6	Sam Brow	40	Male	822.74	5/25/2021

Formatting and Normalizing Data

Ensuring your data is in a consistent and proper format is essential for analysis.

Alex worked on formatting dates and normalizing numeric values, crucial steps to ensure data consistency.

```
# Convert dates to a Date format
customer_data$Registration_Date <-
as.Date(customer_data$Registration_Date, format="%Y-%m-
%d")

# Normalize numeric data
customer_data$Normalized_Age <-
scale(customer_data$Age)
customer_data$Normalized_Purchase_Amount <-
scale(customer_data$Purchase_Amount)

# Verify the changes
head(customer_data)
```

Customer_ID	Name	Age	Gender	Purchase_Amount	Registration_Date	Normalized_Age	Normalized_Purchase_Amount
1	John Doe	36	Male	650.75	6/15/2021	-0.26176004	-0.4148126
2	Jane Smith	22	Female	661.25	12/22/2020	-1.50530481	-0.3659081
3	Alex Johnson	47	Male	958.86	2/9/2021	0.71531085	1.0202306
4	Emily Davis	23	Female	666.2	7/3/2021	-1.41648019	-0.3428531
5	Chris White	55	Male	506.21	1/18/2021	1.42590786	-1.0880174
6	Sam Brown	40	Male	822.74	5/25/2021	0.09353847	0.3862425

Validating Data

Validation involves ensuring the data makes sense and adheres to expected formats and ranges.

```
# Check for outliers in numerical data
boxplot(customer_data$Purchase_Amount, main="Purchase
```

Amount")

Remove outliers if necessary
Q1 <- quantile(customer_data$Purchase_Amount, 0.25)
Q3 <- quantile(customer_data$Purchase_Amount, 0.75)
IQR <- Q3 - Q1
*lower_bound <- Q1 - 1.5 * IQR*
*upper_bound <- Q3 + 1.5 * IQR*

customer_data <- customer_data %>%
 filter(Purchase_Amount >= lower_bound &
Purchase_Amount <= upper_bound)

# Verify the changes
boxplot(customer_data$Purchase_Amount, main="Purchase Amount after Removing Outliers")

Purchase Amount after Removing Outliers

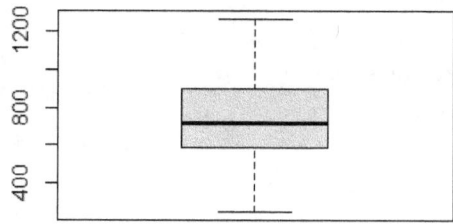

save cleaned customer data
write.csv(customer_data, 'data/cleaned_customer_data.csv')

Conclusion

Data cleaning is a vital step in the data analysis process. By handling missing values, removing duplicates, correcting inconsistencies, and validating your data, you ensure that your analysis is based on accurate and reliable information. Clean data leads to more accurate insights and better decision-making.

Alex leaned back in his chair, satisfied with the clean dataset he had prepared. Lisa reviewed his work and gave an approving nod.

"Great job, Alex," Lisa said. "Now that the data is clean, we can move on to the next stage of analysis."

In the next chapter, we will delve into data manipulation techniques to transform and prepare your data for analysis using R. Alex was ready for the next challenge, eager to apply his newly acquired data cleaning skills to more complex tasks.

Chapter 4: Data Manipulation

After successfully cleaning the dataset, Alex was eager to dive deeper into data manipulation. Lisa, his mentor, approached his desk with a new task.

"Great job on cleaning the data, Alex. Now, let's focus on manipulating this data to prepare it for analysis. Mastering data manipulation techniques will allow you to transform and shape your data to extract valuable insights. Today, we'll cover essential techniques such as filtering, selecting, mutating, summarizing, and joining datasets," Lisa explained.

Alex nodded, ready to get started. He knew that learning these techniques would be crucial for his role as a business analyst at BizTech Solutions.

Introduction

Data manipulation involves transforming and reshaping data to prepare it for analysis. This chapter will guide you through various techniques to manipulate data using R, including filtering rows, selecting columns, creating new variables, summarizing data, and joining datasets.

By the end of this chapter, you will be able to:

1. Filter rows and select columns.

2. Create new variables using mutations.
3. Summarize data with aggregate functions.
4. Join multiple datasets.
5. Reshape data for analysis.

Loading Data

Let's continue using the cleaned dataset from the previous chapter. Ensure that the data is loaded and ready for manipulation.

```
# Load necessary libraries
library(tidyverse)

# Load the cleaned dataset
customer_data <-
read.csv("https://raw.githubusercontent.com/jtmonroe252/D
ata-to-Decisions/main/data/cleaned_customer_data.csv")
%>%
select(-X)

# View the first few rows of the dataset
head(customer_data)
```

Customer_ID	Name	Age	Gender	Purchase_Amount	Registration_Date	Normalized_Age	Normalized_Purchase_Amount
1	John Doe	36	Male	650.75	6/15/2021	-0.26176004	-0.4148126
2	Jane Smith	22	Female	661.25	12/22/2020	-1.50530481	-0.3659081
3	Alex Johnson	47	Male	958.86	2/9/2021	0.71531085	1.0202306
4	Emily Davis	23	Female	666.2	7/3/2021	-1.41648019	-0.3428531
5	Chris White	55	Male	506.21	1/18/2021	1.42590786	-1.0880174
6	Sam Brown	40	Male	822.74	5/25/2021	0.09353847	0.3862425

Filtering Rows

Filtering rows allows you to select a subset of data based on specific conditions. For example, you might want to analyze customers from a particular age group or those who made purchases above a certain amount.

```
# Filter customers who are older than 30
customers_above_30 <- customer_data %>% filter(Age > 30)

# Filter customers with purchase amounts greater than $100
high_value_customers <- customer_data %>%
filter(Purchase_Amount > 100)

# View the filtered data
head(customers_above_30)
```

Customer_ID	Name	Age	Gender	Purchase_Amount	Registration_Date	Normalized_Age	Normalized_Purchase_Amount
1	John Doe	36	Male	650.75	6/15/2021	-0.26176004	-0.41481
3	Alex John	47	Male	958.86	2/9/2021	0.71531085	1.020231
5	Chris Whi	55	Male	506.21	1/18/2021	1.42590786	-1.08802
6	Sam Brow	40	Male	822.74	5/25/2021	0.09353847	0.386243
7	Laura Wil	33	Female	680.54	4/17/2021	-0.52823392	-0.27606
8	Matt Tayl	44	Male	904.24	11/1/2020	0.44883697	0.765834

```
head(high_value_customers)
```

Customer_ID	Name	Age	Gender	Purchase_Amount	Registration_Date	Normalized_Age	Normalized_Purchase_Amount
1	John Doe	36	Male	650.75	6/15/2021	-0.26176004	-0.41481
2	Jane Smit	22	Female	661.25	12/22/2020	-1.50530481	-0.36591
3	Alex John	47	Male	958.86	2/9/2021	0.71531085	1.020231
4	Emily Dav	23	Female	666.2	7/3/2021	-1.41648019	-0.34285
5	Chris Whi	55	Male	506.21	1/18/2021	1.42590786	-1.08802
6	Sam Brow	40	Male	822.74	5/25/2021	0.09353847	0.386243

Selecting Columns

Selecting specific columns is useful when you only need a subset of variables for your analysis.

```
# Select only the Name, Age, and Purchase_Amount columns
selected_columns <- customer_data %>% select(Name, Age,
Purchase_Amount)
```

```
# View the selected columns
head(selected_columns)
```

Name	Age	Purchase_Amount
John Doe	36	650.75
Jane Smith	22	661.25
Alex Johnson	47	958.86
Emily Davis	23	666.2
Chris White	55	506.21
Sam Brown	40	822.74

Creating New Variables

Creating new variables, or mutating, involves adding new columns to your dataset based on transformations of existing columns.

```
# Create a new variable indicating whether the purchase
amount is above the average
# Create a new variable indicating whether the purchase
amount is above the average and Years_as_Customer
average_purchase <-
mean(customer_data$Purchase_Amount)

customer_data <- customer_data %>%
  mutate(Above_Average_Purchase = ifelse(Purchase_Amount
> average_purchase, "Yes", "No")) %>%
  mutate(Customer_Since =
as.POSIXlt(as.Date(Registration_Date)),
      Current = as.POSIXlt(Sys.Date())) %>%
  mutate(Days_as_Customer = Current - Customer_Since)
%>%
  na.omit()

# View the updated dataset
head(customer_data)
```

Customer_ID	Name	Age	Gender	Purchase_Amount	Registration_Date	Normalized_Age	Normalized_Purchase_Amount
1	John Doe	36	Male	650.75	6/15/2021	-0.26176004	-0.41481
2	Jane Smith	22	Female	661.25	12/22/2020	-1.50530481	-0.36591
3	Alex Johnso	47	Male	958.86	2/9/2021	0.71531085	1.020231
4	Emily Davis	23	Female	666.2	7/3/2021	-1.41648019	-0.34285
5	Chris White	55	Male	506.21	1/18/2021	1.42590786	-1.08802
6	Sam Brown	40	Male	822.74	5/25/2021	0.09353847	0.386243

Summarizing Data

Summarizing data helps you calculate aggregate statistics such as the mean, median, count, sum, etc., to gain insights into your dataset.

```
# Summarize the average purchase amount and the number
of customers
summary_stats <- customer_data %>%
  summarise(Average_Purchase = mean(Purchase_Amount),
Total_Customers = n())

# Group by gender and summarize the average purchase
amount and total customers
gender_summary <- customer_data %>%
  group_by(Gender) %>%
  summarise(Average_Purchase = mean(Purchase_Amount),
Total_Customers = n())

# View the summary statistics
summary_stats
```

Average_Purchase	Total_Customers
739.8121	68

gender_summary

Gender	Average_Purchase	Total_Customers
Female	724	23
Male	748	45

Joining Datasets

Joining datasets is essential when you need to combine information from multiple sources. R provides several functions to join datasets, such as inner_join, left_join, right_join, and full_join.

```
# Load additional dataset with customer details
customer_details <-
read.csv("https://raw.githubusercontent.com/jtmonroe252/D
ata-to-Decisions/main/data/customer_details.csv")

# Perform an inner join on the Customer_ID column
merged_data <- customer_data %>%
  inner_join(customer_details, by = "Customer_ID")

# View the merged dataset
head(merged_data)
```

Purchase_Category	Purchase_Channel	Purchase_PaymentType	Amount
Electronics	In-Store	PayPal	40.27
Furniture	Online	Debit Card	53.89
Electronics	Mail Order	Cash	42.92
Groceries	In-Store	Debit Card	84.13
Clothing	In-Store	PayPal	68.33
Clothing	Online	PayPal	42.61

Reshaping Data

Reshaping data involves converting data from a wide format to a long format or vice versa. This is useful for certain types of analysis and visualization.

```
# Convert data from wide to long format
long_data <- customer_data %>%
  pivot_longer(cols = starts_with("Purchase"), names_to =
```

```
"Purchase_Type", values_to = "Amount")

# Convert data from long to wide format
wide_data <- long_data %>%
  pivot_wider(names_from = Purchase_Type, values_from =
Amount)

# View the reshaped data
head(long_data)
head(wide_data)
```

Conclusion

Data manipulation is a powerful skill that allows you to transform and prepare your data for analysis. By filtering rows, selecting columns, creating new variables, summarizing data, and joining datasets, you can shape your data to uncover valuable insights.

Alex leaned back, satisfied with the progress he had made. Lisa reviewed his work and smiled.

"Excellent job, Alex. You've mastered essential data manipulation techniques that will serve you well in your analyses. Next, we'll dive into data visualization to bring your data to life with informative graphics."

In the next chapter, we will explore data visualization techniques to effectively communicate your findings using R. Alex felt confident and ready for the next challenge, eager to see his data come to life through visualization.

Chapter 5: Advanced Statistical Techniques

Alex had become proficient in visualizing data, creating plots that communicated complex insights effectively. Lisa, impressed with his progress, now presented him with a new challenge.

"Alex, you've done a great job with data visualization. Now it's time to dive deeper into advanced statistical techniques. These techniques will allow you to uncover deeper insights and make more informed decisions. Today, we'll cover hypothesis testing, regression analysis, and clustering," Lisa explained.

Alex nodded, ready for the challenge. He knew that mastering these advanced techniques would significantly enhance his analytical capabilities.

Introduction

Advanced statistical techniques are essential for gaining deeper insights from data. These techniques include hypothesis testing, regression analysis, and clustering, among others. In this chapter, you will learn how to perform these analyses using R.

By the end of this chapter, you will be able to:

1. Conduct hypothesis testing to draw inferences from data.
2. Perform regression analysis to model relationships between

variables.

3. Use clustering techniques to segment data into meaningful groups.

Loading Data

Let's continue using the cleaned and manipulated dataset from the previous chapters. Ensure that the data is loaded and ready for analysis.

```
# Load necessary libraries
library(tidyverse)

# Load the cleaned dataset
customer_data <-
read.csv("https://raw.githubusercontent.com/jtmonroe252/
Data-to-Decisions/main/data/cleaned_customer_data.csv")
%>%
select(-X)

# View the first few rows of the dataset
head(customer_data)
```

Customer_ID	Name	Age	Gender	Purchase_Amount	Registration_Date	Normalized_Age	Normalized_Purchase_Amount	Above_Average_Purchase
1	John Doe	36	Male	650.75	6/15/2021	-0.26176004	-0.41481	No
2	Jane Smith	22	Female	661.25	12/22/2020	-1.50530481	-0.36591	No
3	Alex Johnson	47	Male	958.86	2/9/2021	0.71531085	1.020231	Yes
4	Emily Davis	23	Female	666.2	7/3/2021	-1.41648019	-0.34285	No
5	Chris White	55	Male	506.21	1/18/2021	1.42590786	-1.08802	No
6	Sam Brown	40	Male	822.74	5/25/2021	0.09353847	0.386243	Yes

Hypothesis Testing

Hypothesis testing is a statistical method used to make inferences about population parameters based on sample data. It involves testing an assumption regarding a population parameter.

• T-Test

A t-test is used to compare the means of two groups.

```
# Conduct a t-test to compare purchase amounts between
genders
t_test_result <- t.test(Purchase_Amount ~ Gender, data =
customer_data)

# View the t-test result
t_test_result
```

```
Welch Two Sample t-test

data:  Purchase_Amount by Gender
t = -0.46849, df = 52.213, p-value = 0.6414
alternative hypothesis: true difference in means
between group Female and group Male is not equal to
0

95 percent confidence interval:
-129.10801  80.22983

sample estimates:
mean in group Female   mean in group Male
    723.6391               748.0782
```

• Chi-Square Test

A chi-square test is used to examine the association between two
categorical variables.

```
# Conduct a chi-square test to examine the association
between Gender and Above_Average_Purchase
table_data <- table(customer_data$Gender,
customer_data$Above_Average_Purchase)
chi_square_result <- chisq.test(table_data)
```

```
# View the chi-square test result
chi_square_result
```

Pearson's Chi-squared test with Yates' continuity correction
data: table_data
X-squared = 1.4237, df = 1, p-value = 0.2328

Regression Analysis

Regression analysis is a powerful statistical method used to model and analyze the relationships between variables. It helps in understanding how the dependent variable changes when one or more independent variables are varied.

Linear Regression

Linear regression models the relationship between a dependent variable and one or more independent variables using a linear equation.

```
# Fit a linear regression model to predict Purchase_Amount
based on Age and Gender
linear_model <- lm(Purchase_Amount ~ Age + Gender, data =
customer_data)

# View the model summary
summary(linear_model)
```

Call:
lm(formula = Purchase_Amount ~ Age + Gender, data =
customer_data)

Residuals:
Min   1Q   Media   3Q   Max
-456.07 -135.72 -19.47   144.62 526.52

Coefficients:

	Estimate	Std. Error	t value	Pr(>|t|)	
(Intercept)	795.468	99.004	8.035	2.53E-11	***
Age	-1.927	2.364	-0.815	0.418	
GenderMale	29.299	55.827	0.525	0.601	

Signif. codes: 0 '***' 0.001 '**' 0.01 '*' 0.05 '.' 0.1 ' ' 1

Residual standard error: 216.6 on 65 degrees of freedom
Multiple R-squared: 0.01304,
Adjusted R-squared: -0.01733
F-statistic: 0.4292 on 2 and 65 DF, p-value: 0.6528

Multiple Regression

Multiple regression extends linear regression by using multiple independent variables to predict the dependent variable.

```
# Fit a multiple regression model to predict
Purchase_Amount, calculating Days_as_Customer

customer_data %>%
 mutate(Registration_Date = as.Date(Registration_Date)) %>%
 mutate(Days_as_Customer = as.numeric(as.Date("2024-06-11") - Registration_Date)) %>%
 na.omit() -> customer_data

multiple_model <- lm(Purchase_Amount ~ Age + Gender + Days_as_Customer, data = customer_data)

# View the model summary
summary(multiple_model)
```

Call:
lm(formula = Purchase_Amount ~ Age + Gender + Days_as_Customer,
   data = customer_data)

Residuals:
Min   1Q   Median 3Q   Max

-441.16 -125.72 -16.65 134.09 519.12

Coefficients:

	Estimate	Std. Error	t value	Pr(>|t|)	
(Intercept)	836.02208	365.769	2.286	0.0258	*
Age	-2.33434	2.46931	-0.945	0.3482	
GenderMale	47.88716	57.8897	0.827	0.4113	
Days_as_Custo	-0.03062	0.29907	-0.102	0.9188	

Signif. codes: 0 '***' 0.001 '**' 0.01 '*' 0.05 '.' 0.1 ' ' 1

Residual standard error: 218 on 61 degrees of freedom
Multiple R-squared: 0.02203,
Adjusted R-squared: -0.02607
F-statistic: 0.458 on 3 and 61 DF, p-value: 0.7126

Clustering

Clustering is an unsupervised learning technique used to group similar observations into clusters. This technique is useful for segmenting data into meaningful groups.

- **K-Means Clustering**

K-means clustering partitions data into k clusters based on feature similarity.

```
# Scale the data
scaled_data <- scale(customer_data[, c("Age",
"Purchase_Amount", "Days_as_Customer")])

# Determine the optimal number of clusters using the Elbow
method
set.seed(123)
wss <- function(k) {
  kmeans(scaled_data, k, nstart = 10)$tot.withinss
}
k.values <- 1:10
wss_values <- map_dbl(k.values, wss)
```

```
# Plot the Elbow method
plot(k.values, wss_values, type = "b", pch = 19, frame = FALSE,
    xlab = "Number of clusters K",
    ylab = "Total within-clusters sum of squares")
```

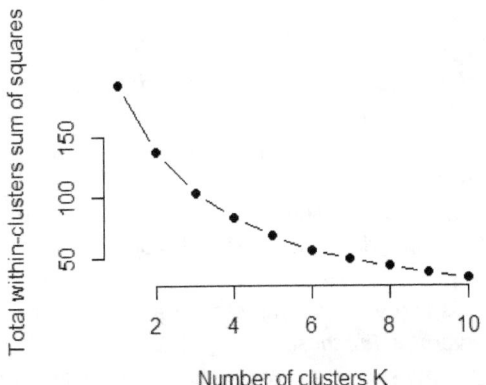

```
# Apply k-means clustering with the optimal number of
clusters (e.g., k = 3)
set.seed(123)
kmeans_result <- kmeans(scaled_data, centers = 3, nstart =
25)
```

```
# Add cluster assignment to the original data
customer_data$Cluster <- kmeans_result$cluster
```

```
# View the clustered data
head(customer_data)
```

Advanced Topics

- **Principal Component Analysis (PCA)**

PCA is used to reduce the dimensionality of data while retaining most of the variation in the dataset.

```
# Perform PCA on the scaled data
pca_result <- prcomp(scaled_data, center = TRUE, scale. =
TRUE)

# View the summary of the PCA result
summary(pca_result)

# Plot the PCA
autoplot(pca_result, data = customer_data, colour = 'Cluster',
label = TRUE, label.size = 3)
```

Logistic Regression
Logistic regression is used for binary classification problems
where the dependent variable is categorical.

```
# Fit a logistic regression model to predict
Above_Average_Purchase
logistic_model <- glm(Above_Average_Purchase ~ Age +
Gender + Purchase_Amount, data = customer_data, family =
"binomial")

# View the model summary
summary(logistic_model)
```

Customer_ID	Name	Age	Gender	Purchase_Amount	Registration_Date	Normalized_Age	Normalized_Purchase_Amount	Above_Average_Purchase	Days_as_Customer	Cluster
1	John Doe	36	Male	650.75	6/15/2021	-0.26176	-0.41481	No	1092	1
2	Jane Smith	22	Female	661.25	12/22/2020	-1.5053	-0.36591	No	1267	1
3	Alex Johnson	47	Male	958.86	2/9/2021	0.715311	1.020231	Yes	1218	2
4	Emily Davis	23	Female	666.2	7/3/2021	-1.41648	-0.34285	No	1074	1
5	Chris White	55	Male	506.21	1/18/2021	1.425908	-1.08802	No	1240	3
6	Sam Brown	40	Male	822.74	5/25/2021	0.093538	0.386243	Yes	1113	2

Conclusion

Advanced statistical techniques are powerful tools that allow you to
extract deeper insights from your data. By mastering hypothesis
testing, regression analysis, and clustering, you can make more
informed decisions and uncover patterns that were not immediately
apparent.

Alex applied these techniques to the dataset, uncovering new insights and gaining a deeper understanding of the data. Lisa reviewed his work and smiled approvingly.

"Excellent work, Alex. You've mastered some of the most important statistical techniques in data analysis. Next, we'll look at applying these techniques to real-world business problems," Lisa said.

In the next chapter, we will explore how to apply advanced statistical techniques to solve real-world business problems. Alex felt confident and ready for the next challenge, eager to see how these powerful tools could drive business success.

Chapter 6: Data Visualization

Alex had successfully mastered data manipulation techniques, and Lisa was impressed with his progress. Now, she approached him with the next challenge: data visualization.

"Great job on manipulating the data, Alex. Now it's time to bring those insights to life with data visualization. Visualizing data helps in understanding complex patterns and communicating findings effectively. Today, we'll explore various visualization techniques using R. You'll learn how to create basic plots, enhance visualizations, and use advanced plotting libraries," Lisa explained.

Excited about the new challenge, Alex eagerly opened his laptop, ready to dive into the world of data visualization.

Introduction

Data visualization is a crucial aspect of data analysis. It allows you to present data in a graphical format, making it easier to identify patterns, trends, and outliers. In this chapter, you will learn how to create various types of visualizations using R, including scatter plots, bar charts, histograms, box plots, and more.

By the end of this chapter, you will be able to:

1. Create basic plots using ggplot2.

2. Customize and enhance visualizations.
3. Use advanced plotting techniques for complex data.
4. Interpret and present your visualizations effectively.

Loading Data

Let's continue using the cleaned and manipulated dataset from the previous chapters. Ensure that the data is loaded and ready for visualization.

```
# Load necessary libraries
library(tidyverse)

# Load the cleaned dataset
customer_data <-
read.csv("https://raw.githubusercontent.com/jtmonroe252/D
ata-to-Decisions/main/data/cleaned_customer_data.csv")
%>%
select(-X)

# View the first few rows of the dataset
head(customer_data)
```

Name	Age	Gender Purc	hase_Amount Reg	istration_Date	Normalized_Age Normaliz	ed_Purchase_ Amount	Above_Av erage_Pur chase
John Doe	36	Male	650.75	6/15/2021	-0.26176	-0.41481	No
Jane Smith	22	Female	661.25	12/22/2020	-1.5053	-0.36591	No
Alex Johnson	47	Male	958.86	2/9/2021	0.715311	1.020231	Yes
Emily Davis	23	Female	666.2	7/3/2021	-1.41648	-0.34285	No
Chris White	55	Male	506.21	1/18/2021	1.425908	-1.08802	No
Sam Brown	40	Male	822.74	5/25/2021	0.093538	0.386243	Yes

Basic Plots

- **Scatter Plot**

Scatter plots are useful for visualizing the relationship between two numerical variables.

```
# Create a scatter plot of Age vs. Purchase_Amount
ggplot(customer_data, aes(x = Age, y = Purchase_Amount)) +
  geom_point() +
  labs(title = "Scatter Plot of Age vs. Purchase Amount", x =
"Age", y = "Purchase Amount")
```

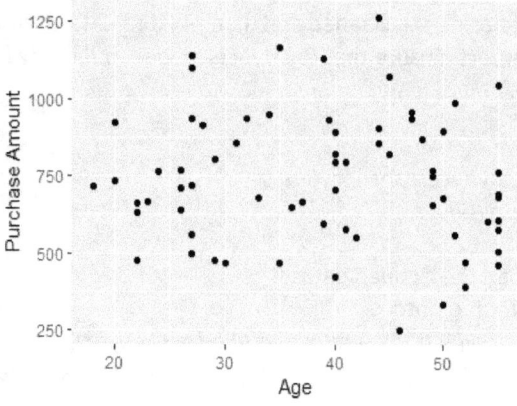

Scatter Plot of Age vs. Purchase Amount

- **Bar Chart**

Bar charts are ideal for comparing categorical data.

```
# Create a bar chart of the number of customers by Gender
ggplot(customer_data, aes(x = Gender)) +
  geom_bar(fill = "skyblue") +
  labs(title = "Bar Chart of Customers by Gender", x =
"Gender", y = "Count")
```

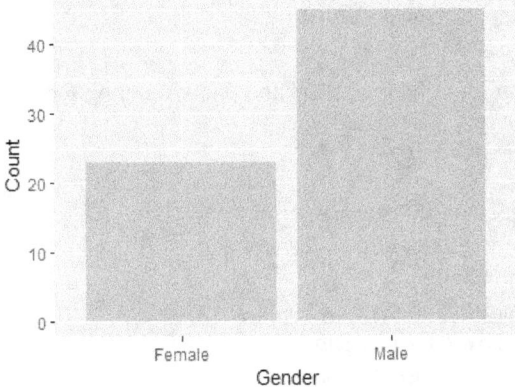

Bar Chart of Customers by Gender

- **Histogram**

Histograms are used to visualize the distribution of a numerical variable.

```
# Create a histogram of Purchase_Amount
ggplot(customer_data, aes(x = Purchase_Amount)) +
  geom_histogram(binwidth = 10, fill = "lightgreen", color =
  "black") +
  labs(title = "Histogram of Purchase Amounts", x = "Purchase
  Amount", y = "Frequency")
```

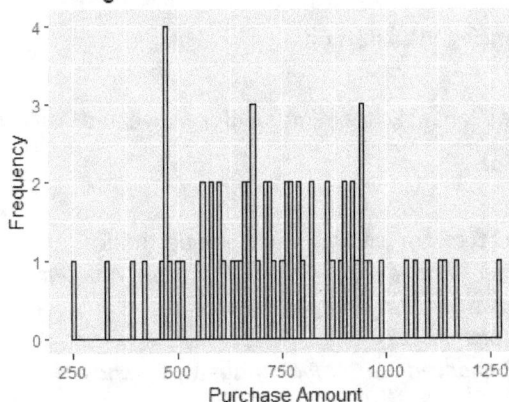

Histogram of Purchase Amounts

- **Box Plot**

Box plots are useful for identifying outliers and understanding the spread of the data.

```
# Create a box plot of Purchase_Amount by Gender
ggplot(customer_data, aes(x = Gender, y =
Purchase_Amount)) +
 geom_boxplot(fill = "lightblue") +
 labs(title = "Box Plot of Purchase Amount by Gender", x =
"Gender", y = "Purchase Amount")
```

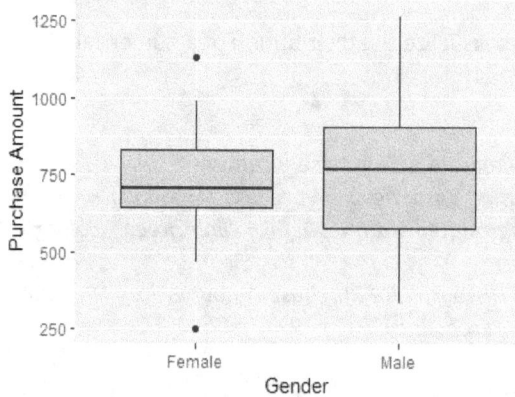

Box Plot of Purchase Amount by Gender

Customizing and Enhancing Visualizations

Enhancing visualizations can make them more informative and visually appealing.

```
# Enhanced scatter plot with color and size aesthetics
ggplot(customer_data, aes(x = Age, y = Purchase_Amount,
color = Gender, size = Purchase_Amount)) +
 geom_point(alpha = 0.7) +
 labs(title = "Enhanced Scatter Plot of Age vs. Purchase
```

Amount", x = "Age", y = "Purchase Amount") +
theme_minimal()

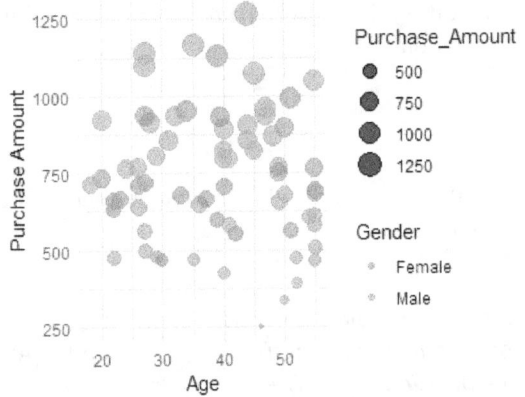

Adding themes and customizing axis labels
ggplot(customer_data, aes(x = Gender, y = Purchase_Amount,
fill = Gender)) +
  geom_boxplot() +
  labs(title = "Box Plot of Purchase Amount by Gender", x =
  "Gender", y = "Purchase Amount") +
  theme_classic() +
  scale_fill_brewer(palette = "Pastel1")

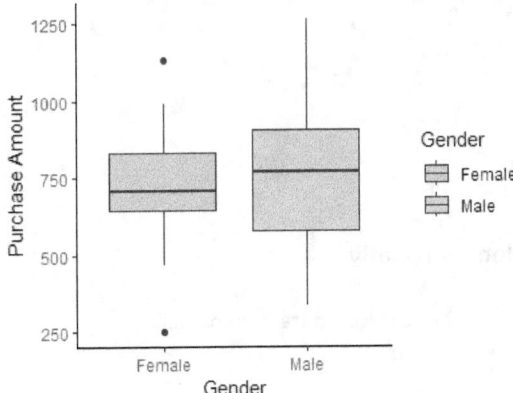

Advanced Plotting Techniques

Using advanced plotting libraries can help create complex and interactive visualizations.

- **Faceted Plots**

Faceted plots are used to split data into multiple panels based on a categorical variable.

```
# Faceted scatter plot by Gender
ggplot(customer_data, aes(x = Age, y = Purchase_Amount)) +
  geom_point(alpha = 0.7) +
  facet_wrap(~ Gender) +
  labs(title = "Faceted Scatter Plot of Age vs. Purchase Amount
by Gender", x = "Age", y = "Purchase Amount")
```

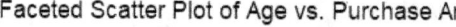

Faceted Scatter Plot of Age vs. Purchase Ar

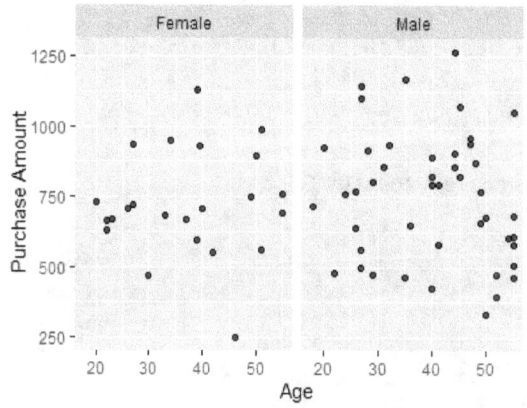

- **Interactive Plots with Plotly**

Interactive plots allow users to explore data dynamically.

```
# Install and load plotly
```

```
install.packages("plotly")
library(plotly)

# Create an interactive scatter plot
p <- ggplot(customer_data, aes(x = Age, y =
Purchase_Amount, color = Gender)) +
  geom_point() +
  labs(title = "Interactive Scatter Plot of Age vs. Purchase
Amount", x = "Age", y = "Purchase Amount")

ggplotly(p)
```

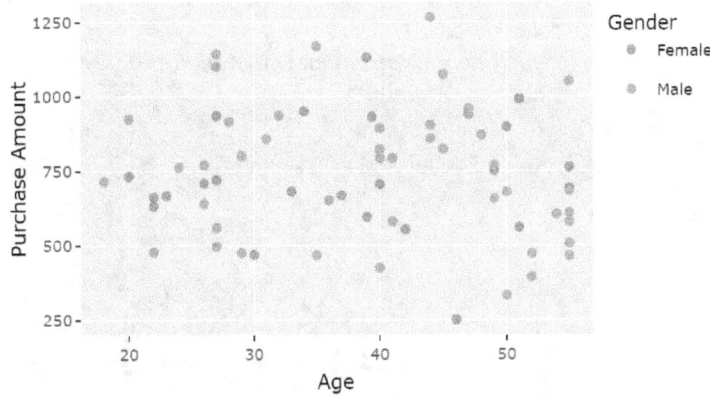

Interactive Scatter Plot of Age vs. Purchase Amount

Interpreting and Presenting Visualizations

Effective data visualization not only involves creating plots but also interpreting and presenting them to communicate insights clearly.

Interpretation Tips

1. Identify Patterns and Trends: Look for relationships between variables, such as correlations or trends over time.
2. Spot Outliers: Use visualizations like box plots to identify data points that deviate significantly from others.
3. Compare Groups: Use bar charts and faceted plots to compare different categories or groups.

Presentation Tips

1. Keep It Simple: Avoid cluttering your visualizations with too many elements. Focus on the key message.
2. Use Annotations: Add text annotations to highlight important points or trends.
3. Consistent Color Schemes: Use consistent colors to represent the same categories across different visualizations.

```
# Adding annotations to a scatter plot
ggplot(customer_data, aes(x = Age, y = Purchase_Amount)) +
  geom_point() +
  annotate("text", x = 35, y = 1000, label = "High spenders",
color = "red") +
  labs(title = "Scatter Plot with Annotations", x = "Age", y =
"Purchase Amount")
```

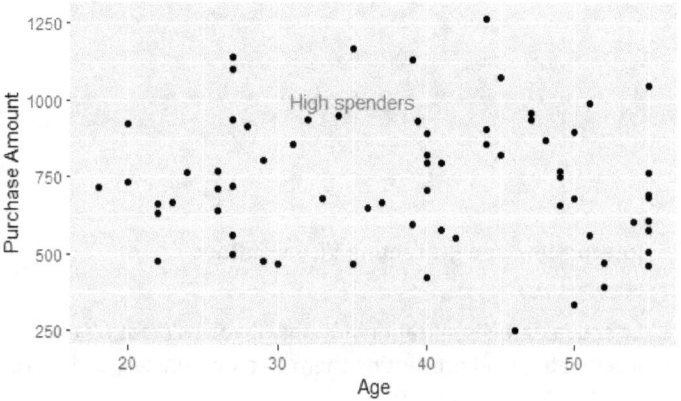

Conclusion

Data visualization is a powerful tool that helps in understanding and communicating complex data. By creating and customizing various types of visualizations, you can effectively convey your insights and findings.

Alex created several visualizations, feeling more confident with each plot. Lisa reviewed his work and nodded in approval.

"Fantastic job, Alex. Your visualizations are clear and informative. Next, we'll move on to performing advanced statistical analysis to derive deeper insights from your data," Lisa said.

In the next chapter, we will explore advanced statistical techniques using R. Alex felt ready to tackle the next challenge, eager to deepen his analytical skills.

Finance Department

Chapter 7: Diving into Financial Data

Alex took a deep breath as he sat down at his new desk in the Finance department. The workspace was neatly organized, with dual monitors and a powerful computer, ready for serious number crunching. Lisa, his mentor, stood by his side, her expression a mix of warmth and expectation.

"Welcome to the Finance department, Alex," Lisa began. "We handle a lot of critical analyses here, from financial forecasting to risk management. Our job is to make sense of the numbers and provide insights that drive the company's strategic decisions."

Alex nodded, eager to get started. "I'm ready to dive in," he said.

"Great," Lisa replied. "Your first task is to analyze historical stock prices and financial statements. We'll start with some basics and gradually move on to more complex analyses. Let's begin by setting up your environment."

Lisa guided Alex through the initial setup, ensuring he had all the necessary software and data. Once everything was in place, she left him to explore and work on the task.

Technical Tutorial: Introduction to Financial Data Analysis with R

Getting Started:

1. Loading Necessary Libraries:

- Load the required libraries for financial data analysis.

   ```
   # Install required packages if not already installed
   install.packages("tidyverse")
   install.packages("quantmod")

   # Load the libraries
   library(tidyverse)
   library(quantmod)
   ```

1. Fetching Historical Stock Data:

- Use the quantmod package to fetch historical stock data for analysis.

   ```
   # Get historical stock data for AAPL, GOOG, and MSFT
   getSymbols(c("AAPL", "GOOG", "MSFT"), from = "2020-01-01", to = "2023-01-01")

   # View the first few rows of the data
   head(AAPL)
   ```

	AAPL.Open	AAPL.High	AAPL.Low	AAPL.Close	AAPL.Volume	AAPL.Adjusted
1/2/2020	74.06	75.15	73.7975	75.0875	1.35E+08	73.05943
1/3/2020	74.2875	75.145	74.125	74.3575	1.46E+08	72.34914
1/6/2020	73.4475	74.99	73.1875	74.95	1.18E+08	72.92561
1/7/2020	74.96	75.225	74.37	74.5975	1.09E+08	72.58266
1/8/2020	74.29	76.11	74.29	75.7975	1.32E+08	73.75023
1/9/2020	76.81	77.6075	76.55	77.4075	1.70E+08	75.31675

   ```
   head(GOOG)
   ```

	GOOG.Open	GOOG.High	GOOG.Low	GOOG.Close	GOOG.Volume	GOOG.Adjusted
1/2/2020	67.0775	68.407	67.0775	68.3685	28132000	68.29079
1/3/2020	67.393	68.625	67.2772	68.033	23728000	67.95567
1/6/2020	67.5	69.825	67.5	69.7105	34646000	69.63126
1/7/2020	69.897	70.1495	69.519	69.667	30054000	69.58781
1/8/2020	69.604	70.579	69.542	70.216	30560000	70.13619
1/9/2020	71.0285	71.3665	70.5135	70.9915	30018000	70.9108

   ```
   head(MSFT)
   ```

	MSFT.Open	MSFT.High	MSFT.Low	MSFT.Close	MSFT.Volume	MSFT.Adjusted
1/2/2020	158.78	160.73	158.33	160.62	22622100	154.4938
1/3/2020	158.32	159.95	158.06	158.62	21116200	152.5701
1/6/2020	157.08	159.1	156.51	159.03	20813700	152.9645
1/7/2020	159.32	159.67	157.32	157.58	21634100	151.5698
1/8/2020	158.93	160.8	157.95	160.09	27746500	153.9841
1/9/2020	161.84	162.22	161.03	162.09	21385000	155.9077

Calculating Daily Returns:

- Calculate daily returns for each stock to analyze their performance.

      # Calculate daily returns
      aapl_returns <- dailyReturn(Cl(AAPL))
      goog_returns <- dailyReturn(Cl(GOOG))
      msft_returns <- dailyReturn(Cl(MSFT))

      # View summary statistics of the returns

      summary(aapl_returns)

Index	daily.returns
Min. :2020-01-02	Min. :-0.1286470
1st Qu.:2020-09-30	1st Qu.:-0.0110315
Median :2021-07-01	Median : 0.0005575
Mean :2021-07-01	Mean : 0.0009954
3rd Qu.:2022-03-31	3rd Qu.: 0.0141512
Max. :2022-12-30	Max. : 0.1198083

      summary(goog_returns)

Index	daily.returns
Min. :2020-01-02	Min. :-0.1110082
1st Qu.:2020-09-30	1st Qu.:-0.0096928
Median :2021-07-01	Median : 0.0011505
Mean :2021-07-01	Mean : 0.0005789
3rd Qu.:2022-03-31	3rd Qu.: 0.0112628
Max. :2022-12-30	Max. : 0.0940166

summary(msft_returns)

Index	daily.returns
Min. :2020-01-02	Min. :-0.1473903
1st Qu.:2020-09-30	1st Qu.:-0.0096778
Median :2021-07-01	Median : 0.0005349
Mean :2021-07-01	Mean : 0.0007700
3rd Qu.:2022-03-31	3rd Qu.: 0.0122270
Max. :2022-12-30	Max. : 0.1421689

1. Visualizing Stock Returns:

- Create a line plot to visualize the daily returns of the stocks.

```
# Create a data frame with the returns
returns_df <- data.frame(
  Date = index(aapl_returns),
  AAPL = coredata(aapl_returns),
  GOOG = coredata(goog_returns),
  MSFT = coredata(msft_returns)
) %>%
  rename("AAPL" = 2, GOOG = 3, MSFT = 4)

# Plot the daily returns
ggplot(returns_df, aes(x = Date)) +
  geom_line(aes(y = AAPL, color = "AAPL")) +
  geom_line(aes(y = GOOG, color = "GOOG")) +
  geom_line(aes(y = MSFT, color = "MSFT")) +
  labs(title = "Daily Returns of AAPL, GOOG, and MSFT", x =
```

"Date", y = "Return")

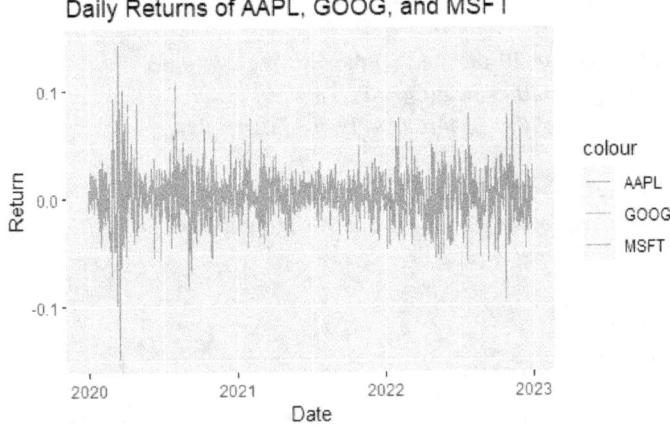

Alex followed Lisa's instructions, typing each command with a mix of anticipation and curiosity. As the code executed and the plots appeared, he felt a sense of accomplishment. The graphs showed the daily returns of the stocks, revealing trends and patterns that were crucial for the financial analysis.

Lisa returned to check on his progress. "How's it going, Alex?"

"It's going well," Alex replied, showing her the plots. "I've calculated the daily returns and visualized them. It's fascinating to see the trends."

"Excellent work," Lisa said, impressed. "Now, let's dive deeper into financial analysis. Next, we'll look at calculating moving averages and volatility, essential for understanding stock performance."

Technical Tutorial: Advanced Financial Data Analysis

Calculating Moving Averages:

Simple Moving Average (SMA):

- Calculate the simple moving average for each stock.

  ```
  # Calculate 20-day and 50-day moving averages
  aapl_sma20 <- SMA(Cl(AAPL), n = 20)
  aapl_sma50 <- SMA(Cl(AAPL), n = 50)

  # Plot the closing prices and moving averages
  chartSeries(AAPL, TA = "addSMA(20);addSMA(50)", theme =
  chartTheme("white"))
  ```

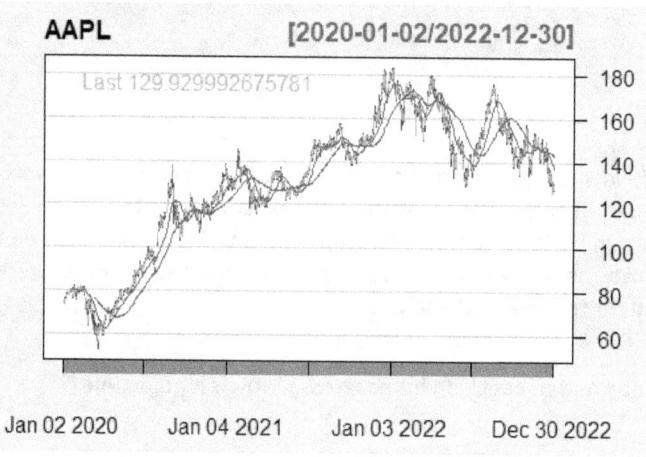

Exponential Moving Average (EMA):

- Calculate the exponential moving average for each stock.

  ```
  # Calculate 20-day and 50-day exponential moving averages
  aapl_ema20 <- EMA(Cl(AAPL), n = 20)
  aapl_ema50 <- EMA(Cl(AAPL), n = 50)

  # Plot the closing prices and exponential moving averages
  chartSeries(AAPL, TA = "addEMA(20);addEMA(50)", theme =
  chartTheme("white"))
  ```

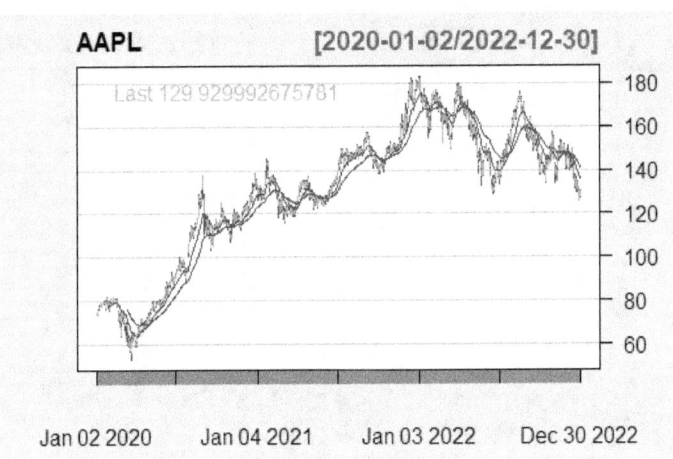

Calculating Volatility:

Volatility Calculation:

- Calculate the volatility of the stock returns.

  # Calculate the rolling standard deviation (volatility)
  aapl_volatility <- runSD(Cl(AAPL), n = 20)

  # Plot the volatility
  chartSeries(aapl_volatility, theme = chartTheme("white"),
  name = "AAPL Volatility (20-day)")

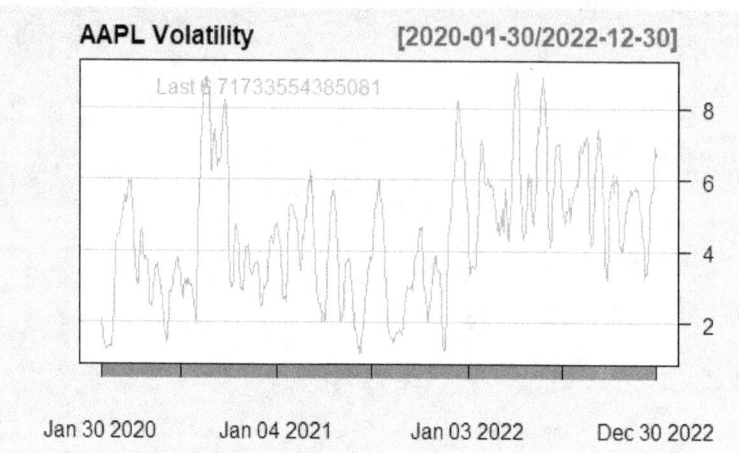

AAPL Volatility [2020-01-30/2022-12-30]

Last 6.71733554385081

By the end of the day, Alex had a comprehensive understanding of financial data analysis using R. He had successfully calculated and visualized moving averages and volatility, gaining insights into stock performance. Lisa reviewed his work and nodded approvingly.

"Fantastic job, Alex. You've got a good grasp of the basics," she said. "Tomorrow, we'll explore more advanced topics like risk management and portfolio optimization. For now, take some time to review what you've learned."

As Alex packed up his things and headed home, he felt a sense of achievement. The day had been productive, and he was eager to continue his journey through the world of business analytics at BizTech Solutions. This was just the beginning, and he was ready for the challenges ahead.

Exercises:

1. Fetching Stock Data:
   - Fetch historical stock data for another company of

your choice.

- ◦ Calculate and visualize its daily returns.

2. Moving Averages:

  - ◦ Calculate the 30-day and 60-day simple moving averages for the new stock.
  - ◦ Plot the stock's closing prices along with the moving averages.

3. Volatility Analysis:

  - ◦ Calculate the 30-day rolling standard deviation (volatility) for the new stock.
  - ◦ Visualize the volatility over time.

By completing these exercises, you'll reinforce your understanding of financial data analysis with R and prepare for more complex analyses in the next chapters. Alex's journey at BizTech Solutions is just beginning, and so is your adventure with R programming in business analytics.

Chapter 8: Time Series Analysis

The next morning, Alex arrived at the office with a renewed sense of excitement. He greeted Lisa, who was already immersed in her work. As he settled in, Lisa approached his desk with a stack of reports and a welcoming smile.

"Good morning, Alex," Lisa said. "Today, we'll be diving into time series analysis. This is crucial for financial forecasting and understanding market trends. Are you ready to get started?"

"Absolutely," Alex replied. "I'm eager to learn."

"Great," Lisa continued. "We'll begin by exploring time series components, then move on to more advanced techniques like ARIMA modeling and forecasting."

Technical Tutorial: Introduction to Time Series Analysis

Understanding Time Series Components

Loading and Preparing Data

Start by loading historical stock price data and preparing it for analysis.

```
# Load necessary libraries
library(quantmod)
library(forecast)
library(ggplot2)

# Get historical stock data for GOOG
getSymbols("GOOG", src = "yahoo", from = "2010-01-01", to = "2023-
01-01")
goog_prices <- Cl(GOOG)

# Plot the data
autoplot(goog_prices, main = "Google Stock Prices") +
  ylab("Price") + xlab("Time")
```

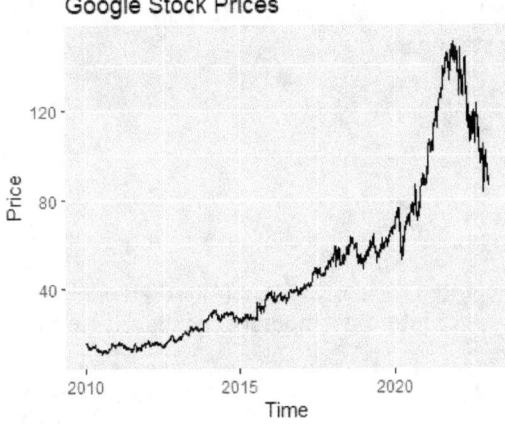

Checking for Stationarity

To ensure the time series is stationary, perform the Augmented
Dickey-Fuller (ADF) test.

```
# Perform ADF test
adf_test <- adf.test(goog_prices)
print(adf_test)
```

Augmented Dickey-Fuller Test

data: goog_prices
Dickey-Fuller = -1.8076, Lag order = 14, p-value = 0.6598
alternative hypothesis: stationary

If the series is not stationary, difference the data
goog_diff <- diff(goog_prices, differences = 1)
adf_test_diff <- adf.test(goog_diff)
print(adf_test_diff)

Augmented Dickey-Fuller Test

data: goog_diff
Dickey-Fuller = -15.588, Lag order = 14, p-value = 0.01
alternative hypothesis: stationary

Model Selection

ARIMA Model

The AutoRegressive Integrated Moving Average (ARIMA) model is used for its effectiveness in capturing temporal dependencies in the stock prices.

Fit ARIMA model
goog_arima <- auto.arima(goog_prices)
summary(goog_arima)

Augmented Dickey-Fuller Test

data: goog_diff
Dickey-Fuller = -15.588, Lag order = 14, p-value = 0.01
alternative hypothesis: stationary

goog_arima <- auto.arima(goog_prices)

summary(goog_arima)

Series: goog_prices
ARIMA(1,1,1)

Coefficients:
     ar1   ma1
    0.7174 -0.7667
s.e. 0.1026 0.0945

sigma^2 = 1.264: log likelihood = -5023.13
AIC=10052.27 AICc=10052.27 BIC=10070.55

Training set error measures:

	ME	RMSE	MAE	MPE	MAPE	MASE	ACF1
Training set	0.0271	1.123629	0.6091345	0.04729366	1.157043	1.001388	-0.01065

Forecast using ARIMA
goog_forecast_arima <- forecast(goog_arima, h = 30)
autoplot(goog_forecast_arima, main = "Google Stock Price Forecast using ARIMA")

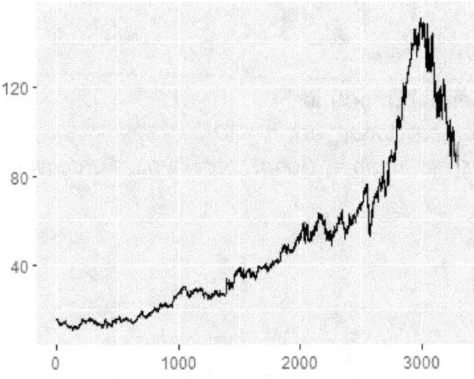

Exponential Smoothing

Exponential smoothing methods are also employed for comparison, leveraging their simplicity and ability to handle trends.

```
# Fit Exponential Smoothing model
goog_ets <- ets(goog_prices)
summary(goog_ets)
```

ETS(M,N,N)

Call:
 ets(y = goog_prices)

 Smoothing parameters:
  alpha = 0.9551

 Initial states:
  l = 15.6043

 sigma: 0.017

   AIC   AICc   BIC
23602.90 23602.90 23621.17

Training set error measures:

	ME	RMSE	MAE	MPE	MAPE	MASE	ACF1
Training set	0.0234	1.12473	0.608394	0.04057502	1.155016	1.000171	-0.01192

```
# Forecast using Exponential Smoothing
goog_forecast_ets <- forecast(goog_ets, h = 30)
autoplot(goog_forecast_ets, main = "Google Stock Price Forecast using
ETS")
```

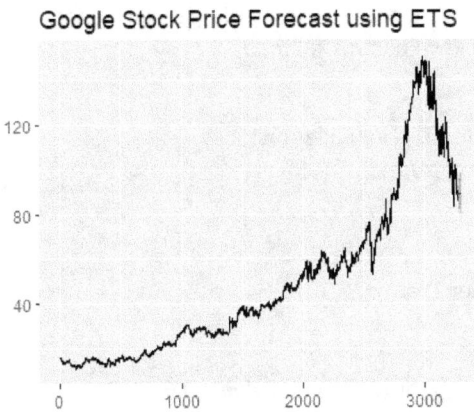

Google Stock Price Forecast using ETS

Performance Evaluation

The models' performances are evaluated based on prediction accuracy, comparing forecasted values with actual stock prices.

Alex carefully followed the instructions, typing each command and observing the output. The decomposition plot revealed the underlying trend, seasonal patterns, and residuals in the stock prices. Lisa looked over his shoulder, nodding in approval.

"Understanding these components is essential," Lisa explained. "It helps us identify patterns and make more accurate forecasts. Now, let's move on to ARIMA modeling, a powerful tool for time series forecasting."

Technical Tutorial: ARIMA Modeling

1. Checking Stationarity

Before building an ARIMA model, ensure the time series is stationary. Use the Augmented Dickey-Fuller (ADF) test.

```
# Perform the Augmented Dickey-Fuller test
adf_test <- adf.test(goog_prices)
print(adf_test)
```

Augmented Dickey-Fuller Test

data: goog_prices
Dickey-Fuller = -1.8076, Lag order = 14, p-value = 0.6598
alternative hypothesis: stationary

2. Differencing the Time Series

If the series is not stationary, difference it to achieve stationarity.

```
# Difference the series to make it stationary
goog_diff <- diff(goog_prices, differences = 1)
```

```
# Plot the differenced series
plot(goog_diff, main = "Differenced GOOG Closing Prices")
```

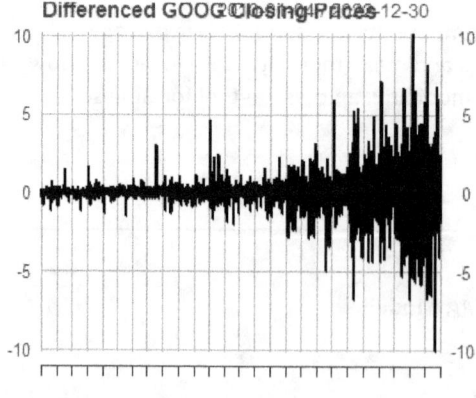

3. Building the ARIMA Model

Fit an ARIMA model to the differenced time series.

Fit the ARIMA model
goog_arima <- auto.arima(goog_diff)

Print the model summary
summary(goog_arima)

Series: goog_diff
ARIMA(1,0,1) with zero mean

Coefficients:

	ar1	ma1
	0.7174	-0.7667
s.e.	0.1026	0.0945

sigma^2 = 1.264: log likelihood = -5023.13
AIC=10052.27 AICc=10052.27 BIC=10070.55

Training set error measures:

	ME	RMSE	MAE	MPE	MAPE	MASE	ACF1
Training se	0.02710148	1.123801	0.609316	-9.845981	565.9481	0.676481	-0.01065

4. Forecasting with ARIMA

Use the fitted ARIMA model to make forecasts.

Forecast the next 30 days
goog_forecast <- forecast(goog_arima, h = 30)

Plot the forecast
plot(goog_forecast, main = "GOOG 30-Day Forecast")

GOOG 30-Day Forecast

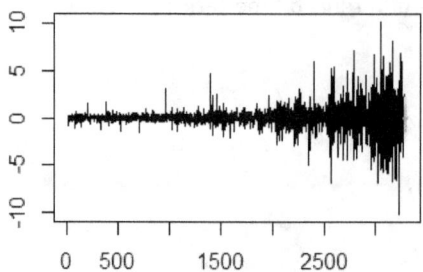

As Alex executed the commands, the forecast plot displayed potential future prices for GOOG. The process was intricate but incredibly insightful. He felt a growing sense of competence as he navigated through the complexities of time series analysis.

Lisa reviewed his work once again. "Well done, Alex. You've got a good handle on the basics of ARIMA modeling. Tomorrow, we'll look at more advanced topics like volatility forecasting and GARCH models. For now, take some time to review what you've learned."

As Alex packed up his things and prepared to leave, he reflected on the day's lessons. The world of financial forecasting was complex, but with each step, he felt more confident in his abilities. The journey through BizTech Solutions was proving to be both challenging and rewarding, and he was eager to see what the next day would bring.

Exercises:

1. **Decomposing Time Series**: Decompose the time series of another stock (e.g., GOOG) and plot the components.
2. **Stationarity Check**: Perform the ADF test on the new stock's

closing prices and interpret the results.

3. **Building ARIMA Models**: Fit an ARIMA model to the new stock's time series and summarize the model.

4. **Forecasting**: Generate and plot a 30-day forecast for the new stock using the fitted ARIMA model.

By completing these exercises and following along with Alex's journey, you'll gain a deeper understanding of time series analysis and forecasting in R, setting a solid foundation for more advanced financial analytics. Alex's adventure at BizTech Solutions continues, and so does your learning path in R programming and business analytics.

Chapter 9: Financial Calculations and Analysis

The next morning, Alex walked into the office, ready for another day of learning. Lisa was already at her desk, preparing materials for their next session. She looked up and greeted him with a smile.

"Good morning, Alex. Today, we'll dive into some financial calculations and analysis. This will give you a solid foundation for understanding financial metrics and their applications in business."

"Sounds great, Lisa. I'm ready to learn."

"Excellent. We'll start with some basic financial ratios and then move on to more complex analyses."

Technical Tutorial: Financial Calculations and Analysis

Loading and Preparing Data

We will begin by loading financial data for Google (GOOG) and preparing it for analysis.

```r
# Load necessary libraries
library(quantmod)
library(dplyr)

# Get financial data for GOOG
getSymbols("GOOG", src = "yahoo", from = "2010-01-01", to = "2023-01-01")
goog_data <- as.data.frame(GOOG) %>%
  rownames_to_column(var="Date") %>%
  mutate(Date = as.Date(Date))

# Extract the necessary columns for analysis
goog_prices <- goog_data %>% select(Date, GOOG.Adjusted)
```

Calculating Financial Ratios

Financial ratios are crucial for evaluating a company's performance. We'll start with some basic ratios.

Price-to-Earnings (P/E) Ratio

The P/E ratio measures a company's current share price relative to its per-share earnings.

```r
# Calculate P/E Ratio
# Assuming 'earnings_per_share' is a known constant for simplicity
earnings_per_share <- 5.0  # Placeholder value
pe_ratio <- goog_prices$GOOG.Adjusted / earnings_per_share

# Add P/E ratio to the data frame
goog_prices <- goog_prices %>% mutate(PE_Ratio = GOOG.Adjusted / earnings_per_share)

# Plot P/E Ratio
plot(goog_prices$Date, goog_prices$PE_Ratio, type = "l", col = "blue",
     main = "GOOG P/E Ratio Over Time", xlab = "Date", ylab = "P/E Ratio")
```

Dividend Yield

The dividend yield shows how much a company pays out in dividends each year relative to its share price.

```
# Calculate Dividend Yield
# Assuming 'dividend_per_share' is a known constant for simplicity
dividend_per_share <- 2.0  # Placeholder value
dividend_yield <- dividend_per_share / goog_prices$GOOG.Adjusted

# Add Dividend Yield to the data frame
goog_prices <- goog_prices %>% mutate(Dividend_Yield =
dividend_per_share / GOOG.Adjusted)

# Plot Dividend Yield
plot(goog_prices$Date, goog_prices$Dividend_Yield, type = "l", col =
"green",
    main = "GOOG Dividend Yield Over Time", xlab = "Date", ylab =
"Dividend Yield")
```

Advanced Financial Analysis

Next, we'll move on to more complex financial analyses like calculating the Weighted Average Cost of Capital (WACC) and Discounted Cash Flow (DCF) analysis.

Weighted Average Cost of Capital (WACC)

WACC represents a firm's cost of capital, where each category of capital is proportionately weighted.

```
# WACC Calculation
# Assumptions for simplicity
cost_of_equity <- 0.08  # 8% cost of equity
cost_of_debt <- 0.04    # 4% cost of debt
```

```
tax_rate <- 0.21      # 21% tax rate
equity_market_value <- 1000000000  # Placeholder value
debt_market_value <- 500000000    # Placeholder value
total_market_value <- equity_market_value + debt_market_value

# WACC formula
wacc <- (equity_market_value / total_market_value) * cost_of_equity
+
    (debt_market_value / total_market_value) * cost_of_debt * (1 -
tax_rate)

print(paste("WACC:", round(wacc, 4)))
```

"WACC: 0.0639"

Discounted Cash Flow (DCF) Analysis

DCF is a valuation method used to estimate the value of an investment based on its expected future cash flows.

```
# DCF Calculation
# Assumptions for simplicity
free_cash_flow <- 20000000  # Placeholder value for the first year
growth_rate <- 0.03       # 3% growth rate
years <- 5                # Forecasting for 5 years

# Calculate present value of cash flows
dcf <- sum(sapply(1:years, function(t) {
  free_cash_flow * (1 + growth_rate)^(t-1) / (1 + wacc)^t
}))

print(paste("DCF Value:", round(dcf, 2)))
```

"DCF Value: 88199734.11"

As Alex executed the commands, he observed how the financial ratios and calculations provided insights into Google's financial health and valuation. Lisa looked over his shoulder, nodding in approval.

"These calculations are fundamental for financial analysis," Lisa explained. "They help us understand the company's performance and make informed investment decisions. Tomorrow, we'll dive into portfolio management and optimization techniques."

Alex felt a growing sense of competence as he navigated through the intricacies of financial analysis. The journey through BizTech Solutions was proving to be both challenging and rewarding, and he was eager to see what the next day would bring.

Exercises:

1. **P/E Ratio**: Calculate and plot the P/E ratio for another stock (e.g., MSFT).
2. **Dividend Yield**: Calculate and plot the dividend yield for the new stock.
3. **WACC Calculation**: Perform a WACC calculation for a hypothetical company with different parameters.
4. **DCF Analysis**: Conduct a DCF analysis for the new stock, assuming different growth rates and cash flows.

By completing these exercises and following along with Alex's journey, you'll gain a deeper understanding of traditional financial calculations and analysis in R, setting a solid foundation for more advanced financial analytics. Alex's adventure at BizTech Solutions continues, and so does your learning path in R programming and business analytics.

Marketing Department

Chapter 10: Understanding Customer Behavior

Alex arrived at BizTech Solutions eager to embrace the new challenges ahead. The Finance department had been a rigorous but rewarding experience, and today marked his first day in the dynamic Marketing department. The department buzzed with creativity and energy, contrasting the more structured atmosphere of Finance.

As he entered the open office space, he was greeted by colorful charts, campaign posters, and a team deeply immersed in discussions. Emily, the head of the Marketing department, approached him with a welcoming smile.

"Welcome to Marketing, Alex," she said warmly. "We have a lot of exciting projects that require your analytical skills. Today, we'll focus on understanding customer behavior through segmentation. Ready to dive in?"

"Absolutely," Alex replied with enthusiasm.

Emily led Alex to his new workspace, where a computer loaded with customer data awaited. "We'll start by exploring our customer database. Understanding different customer segments helps us tailor our marketing strategies more effectively."

Technical Tutorial: Customer Segmentation Using Clustering in R

1. Loading and Preparing Data:

1. Load the necessary libraries and dataset:

```
# Install required packages if not already installed
install.packages("tidyverse")
install.packages("cluster")
install.packages("factoextra")

# Load the libraries
library(tidyverse)
library(cluster)
library(factoextra)

# Load the cleaned dataset
customer_data <-
read.csv("https://raw.githubusercontent.com/jtmonroe252/D
ata-to-Decisions/main/data/cleaned_customer_data.csv")
%>%
select(-X)

# View the first few rows of the dataset
head(customer_data)
```

Name	Age	Gender	Purchase_Amount	Registration_Date	Normalized_Age	Normalized_Purchase_Amount
John Doe	36	Male	650.75	6/15/2021	-0.26176004	-0.41481
Jane Smith	22	Female	661.25	12/22/2020	-1.50530481	-0.36591
Alex Johnson	47	Male	958.86	2/9/2021	0.71531085	1.020231
Emily Davis	23	Female	666.2	7/3/2021	-1.41648019	-0.34285
Chris White	55	Male	506.21	1/18/2021	1.42590786	-1.08802
Sam Brown	40	Male	822.74	5/25/2021	0.09353847	0.386243

1. Data Cleaning and Preprocessing:

```
# Check for missing values
sum(is.na(customer_data))

# Remove rows with missing values
```

```
customer_data <- na.omit(customer_data)

# Remove rows with missing values
customer_data <- na.omit(customer_data)

customer_data %>%
  select(Customer_ID, Normalized_Age,
Normalized_Purchase_Amount) -> customer_data

# Scale the data
scaled_data <- scale(customer_data[, -1]) # Assuming the
first column is customer ID
```

2. K-Means Clustering:

1. Determine the optimal number of clusters using the Elbow
   method:

```
# Calculate the total within-cluster sum of square (WSS) for
different numbers of clusters
wss <- function(k) {
  kmeans(scaled_data, k, nstart = 10)$tot.withinss
}

# Plot the Elbow method
k.values <- 1:10
wss_values <- map_dbl(k.values, wss)

plot(k.values, wss_values, type = "b", pch = 19, frame = FALSE,
    xlab = "Number of clusters K",
    ylab = "Total within-clusters sum of squares")
```

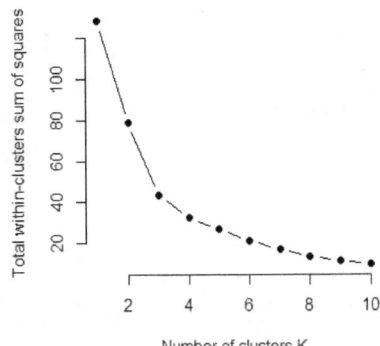

1. Apply K-Means Clustering:

```
# Apply k-means with the optimal number of clusters (e.g., k
= 3)
set.seed(123)
kmeans_result <- kmeans(scaled_data, centers = 3, nstart =
25)

# Add cluster assignment to the original data
customer_data$Cluster <- kmeans_result$cluster

# View the data with cluster assignments
head(customer_data)
```

Customer_ID	Normalized_Age	Normalized_Purchase_Amount	Cluster
1	-0.26176	-0.41481	1
2	-1.5053	-0.36591	1
3	0.715311	1.020231	3
4	-1.41648	-0.34285	1
5	1.425908	-1.08802	2
6	0.093538	0.386243	3

3. Visualizing Clusters:

```
# Visualize the clusters using factoextra
fviz_cluster(kmeans_result, data = scaled_data,
        palette = "jco",
        geom = "point",
        ellipse.type = "convex",
        ggtheme = theme_minimal())
```

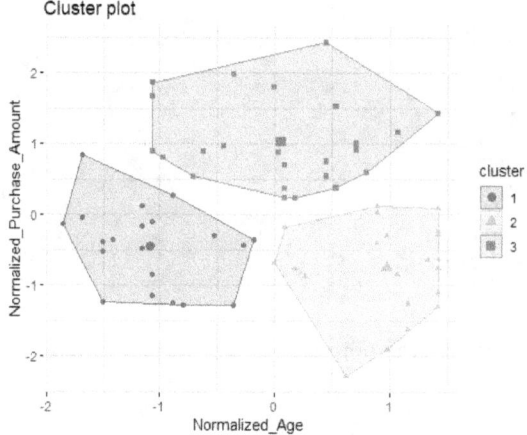

Alex followed the instructions meticulously, his screen displaying a series of colorful plots and charts. The clusters provided clear insights into different customer segments. Emily observed his progress, her excitement palpable.

"Excellent work, Alex," Emily said. "Understanding these segments allows us to create targeted marketing campaigns, improving our outreach and engagement. Let's take it a step further and perform a more detailed analysis of each segment."

Technical Tutorial: Detailed Analysis of Customer Segments

1. Summary Statistics for Each Cluster:

```
# Calculate summary statistics for each cluster
```

```
Customer_clusters <- customer_data %>%
  select(-Customer_ID) %>%
  group_by(Cluster) %>%
  summarise(across(everything(), list(mean = mean, sd = sd)))
```

2. Profiling Each Segment:

```
# Profiling based on cluster means
cluster_profiles <- customer_data %>%
  group_by(Cluster) %>%
  summarise_all(list(mean = mean))

print(cluster_profiles)
```

Cluster	Customer_ID_ mean	Normalized_Age_me an	Normalized_Purcha se_Amount_mean
1	33.6	-1.08	-0.438
2	37.9	0.978	-0.74
3	32	0.058	1.04

3. Visualizing Segment Profiles:

```
# Visualize the profiles of each cluster
customer_data_long <- customer_data %>%
  select(-Customer_ID) %>%
  pivot_longer(cols = -Cluster, names_to = "Variable",
values_to = "Value")

ggplot(customer_data_long, aes(x = Variable, y = Value, fill =
factor(Cluster))) +
  geom_boxplot() +
  facet_wrap(~Cluster) +
  theme_minimal() +
  labs(title = "Customer Segment Profiles", x = "Variable", y =
"Value", fill = "Cluster") +
```

theme(axis.text.x = element_text(angle = 90, vjust = 0.5, hjust=1))

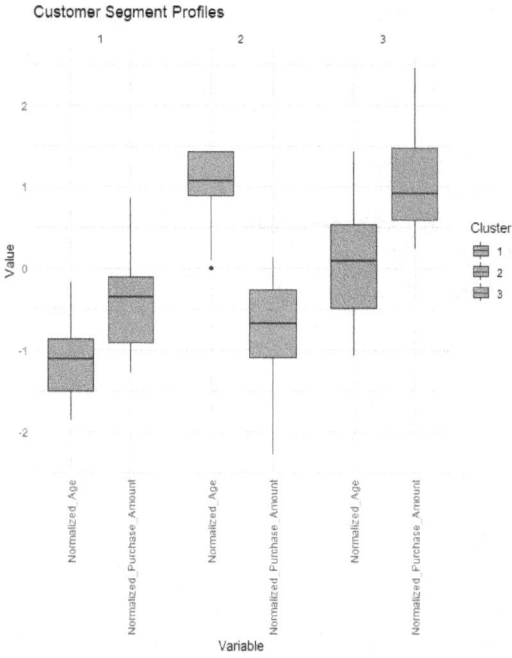

The detailed analysis provided a deeper understanding of each customer segment. Alex could see how different groups exhibited distinct behaviors and preferences. Emily was impressed with his thorough approach and ability to translate complex data into actionable insights.

"Fantastic job, Alex," she said. "These insights will significantly enhance our marketing strategies. Tomorrow, we'll explore A/B testing to measure the effectiveness of our campaigns."

As the day concluded, Alex felt a sense of accomplishment. He had delved into the intricate world of customer behavior, uncovering valuable insights through clustering and profiling. The Marketing department's vibrant atmosphere and the challenging tasks ahead filled him with anticipation for the next chapter in his journey at BizTech Solutions.

Exercises:

1. Cluster Analysis:

   - Perform K-Means clustering on a different dataset and determine the optimal number of clusters.
   - Visualize the clusters and interpret the results.

2. Segment Profiling:

   - Calculate summary statistics for each cluster in your new dataset.
   - Visualize the profiles of each segment and identify key characteristics.

3. Advanced Clustering:

   - Experiment with different clustering algorithms such as hierarchical clustering.
   - Compare the results with K-Means clustering and analyze the differences.

By completing these exercises and following along with Alex's journey, you'll gain a comprehensive understanding of customer segmentation and profiling using R, equipping you with the skills to make data-driven decisions in marketing. Alex's adventure at BizTech Solutions continues, and so does your learning path in R programming and business analytics.

Chapter 11: A/B Testing and Campaign Analysis

The next day, Alex arrived at the Marketing department eager to delve deeper into the world of customer behavior and campaign effectiveness. Emily greeted him with her usual enthusiasm, a stack of reports in hand.

"Good morning, Alex. Today, we'll explore A/B testing, a crucial technique for measuring the effectiveness of our marketing campaigns. We'll start with the basics and move on to analyzing real campaign data. Are you ready?"

"Absolutely," Alex replied. "I'm excited to learn more."

Emily led him to a conference room where a presentation was set up. "A/B testing helps us compare two versions of a campaign to see which one performs better. This could be anything from email subject lines to website layouts. Let's dive in."

Technical Tutorial: A/B Testing with R

1. Understanding A/B Testing:

- A/B testing involves randomly splitting your audience into two groups: A (control) and B (treatment). You then compare the performance of these groups to determine which version is more effective.

2. Loading and Preparing Data:

```
# Install and load necessary libraries
install.packages("tidyverse")
install.packages("broom")

library(tidyverse)
library(broom)

# Load the A/B test dataset
ab_test_data <-
read.csv("https://raw.githubusercontent.com/jtmonroe252/Data-to-Decisions/main/data/ab_test_data.csv")

# View the first few rows of the dataset
head(ab_test_data)
```

User_ID	Group	Metric1	Metric2	Metric3	Converted
1	A	29.5	331	259.5	0
2	B	40.65	398	190.75	0
3	A	35.93	355	310	1
4	B	38.44	306	125.9	0
5	A	9.58	103	480.2	0
6	B	27.26	181	640.75	0

3. Descriptive Statistics:

```
# Summarize the data
summary(ab_test_data)
```

User_ID	Group	Metric1	Metric2	Metric3	Converted
Min. : 1	Length:65	Min. : 9.58	Min. :101.0	Min. :125.9	Min. :0.0000
1st Qu.:17	Class :character	1st Qu.:23.66	1st Qu.:189.0	1st Qu.:299.4	1st Qu.:0.0000
Median :33	Mode :character	Median :29.50	Median :255.0	Median :405.0	Median :0.0000
Mean :33		Mean :33.17	Mean :254.8	Mean :419.5	Mean :0.3846
3rd Qu.:49		3rd Qu.:40.65	3rd Qu.:322.0	3rd Qu.:500.0	3rd Qu.:1.0000
Max. :65		Max. :82.43	Max. :398.0	Max. :850.0	Max. :1.0000

```
# Calculate conversion rates for each group
ab_test_data %>%
  group_by(Group) %>%
  summarise(Conversion_Rate = mean(Converted) * 100) ->
ab_test_data
```

Group	Conversion_Rate
A	42.4
B	34.4

4. Visualizing the Data:

```
# Plot conversion rates
ggplot(ab_test_data, aes(x = Group, y = Converted)) +
  geom_bar(stat = "summary", fun = "mean", fill = "skyblue") +
  labs(title = "Conversion Rates by Group", x = "Group", y =
  "Conversion Rate") +
  theme_minimal()
```

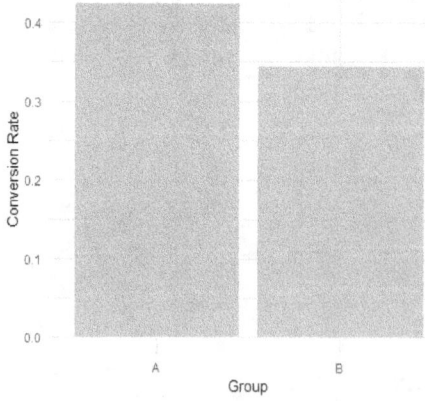

5. Hypothesis Testing:

1. Performing a t-test:

```
# Perform a t-test to compare conversion rates
t_test_result <- t.test(Converted ~ Group, data =
ab_test_data)

# View the t-test results
tidy(t_test_result) %>%
pivot_longer(
  cols = c(estimate, estimate1, estimate2, statistic, p.value,
parameter, conf.low, conf.high),
  names_to = "metric",
  values_to = "value"
)
```

method	alternative	metric	value
Welch Two Sample t-test	two.sided	estimate	0.0805
Welch Two Sample t-test	two.sided	estimate1	0.424
Welch Two Sample t-test	two.sided	estimate2	0.344
Welch Two Sample t-test	two.sided	statistic	0.659
Welch Two Sample t-test	two.sided	p.value	0.512
Welch Two Sample t-test	two.sided	parameter	63
Welch Two Sample t-test	two.sided	conf.low	-0.164
Welch Two Sample t-test	two.sided	conf.high	0.325

1. Interpreting the Results:

- Check the p-value to determine if there is a statistically significant difference between the two groups. A p-value less than 0.05 typically indicates a significant difference.

Alex carefully executed each step, his screen displaying the results of the A/B test. The bar plot clearly showed the difference in conversion rates between the control and treatment groups. The t-test results indicated a statistically significant improvement in the treatment group.

"Great work, Alex," Emily said, reviewing the results. "It looks like our new campaign strategy is more effective. Let's take this a step further by analyzing different metrics and running more sophisticated tests."

Technical Tutorial: Advanced A/B Testing and Campaign Analysis

1. Analyzing Multiple Metrics:

ab_test_data <-
read.csv("https://raw.githubusercontent.com/jtmonroe252/Data-to-Decisions/main/data/ab_test_data.csv")

```
# View the first few rows of the dataset
head(ab_test_data)
```

User_ID	Group	Metric1	Metric2	Metric3	Converted
1	A	29.5	331	259.5	0
2	B	40.65	398	190.75	0
3	A	35.93	355	310	1
4	B	38.44	306	125.9	0
5	A	9.58	103	480.2	0
6	B	27.26	181	640.75	0

```
# Summarize the data by group
ab_test_metrics %>%
  group_by(Group) %>%
  summarise_at(vars(Metric1, Metric2, Metric3), list(mean = mean, sd = sd))
```

Group	Metric1_mean	Metric2_mean	Metric3_mean	Metric1_sd	Metric2_sd	Metric3_sd
A	33.1	253	414	13.9	88.4	140
B	33.3	256	425	16.9	87.6	165

2. Visualizing Multiple Metrics:

```
# Plot multiple metrics by group
ab_test_metrics_long <- ab_test_metrics %>%
  pivot_longer(cols = Metric1:Metric3, names_to = "Metric",
values_to = "Value")

ggplot(ab_test_metrics_long, aes(x = Group, y = Value, fill =
Group)) +
  geom_boxplot() +
  facet_wrap(~ Metric, scales = "free") +
  labs(title = "A/B Test Metrics by Group", x = "Group", y =
"Value") +
  theme_minimal()
```

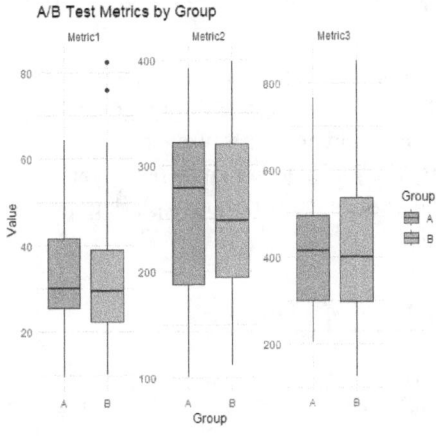

3. Running Multiple Tests:

```
# Perform t-tests for multiple metrics
t_test_results <- ab_test_metrics_long %>%
  group_by(Metric) %>%
  summarise(t_test = list(tidy(t.test(Value ~ Group))))
```

```
# View the t-test results
t_test_results %>%
    unnest(t_test)
```

Metric	estimate	estimate1	estimate2	statistic	p.value	parameter	conf.low	conf.high	method	alternative
Metric1	-0.209	33.1	33.3	-0.0543	0.957	60.1	-7.89	7.47	Welch Two	two.sided
Metric2	-2.83	253	256	-0.129	0.897	63	-46.4	40.8	Welch Two	two.sided
Metric3	-10.4	414	425	-0.274	0.785	60.8	-86.3	65.5	Welch Two	two.sided

The advanced analysis provided a comprehensive view of the campaign's performance across multiple metrics. Alex felt a growing sense of proficiency as he navigated through the various tests and visualizations.

Emily was impressed. "You've done an excellent job, Alex. Understanding these metrics and their implications is crucial for optimizing our marketing strategies. Tomorrow, we'll explore market basket analysis to uncover patterns in customer purchasing behavior."

As the day concluded, Alex felt a profound sense of achievement. He had delved deep into the world of A/B testing and campaign analysis, uncovering valuable insights that would help optimize BizTech Solutions' marketing strategies. The journey was challenging yet immensely rewarding, and he was eager to continue exploring the intricacies of marketing analytics.

Exercises:

1. Basic A/B Testing:

    ◦ Load a new A/B test dataset and perform descriptive statistics.
    ◦ Visualize the conversion rates and run a t-test to compare the groups.

2. Advanced A/B Testing:

   - Analyze multiple metrics from the new dataset.
   - Visualize the data using box plots and run multiple t-tests to compare the groups.

3. Custom Analysis:

   - Design your own A/B test with a hypothetical dataset.
   - Perform and visualize the analysis, interpreting the results.

By completing these exercises and following along with Alex's journey, you'll gain a comprehensive understanding of A/B testing and campaign analysis using R. This chapter equips you with the skills to measure and optimize marketing strategies effectively. Alex's adventure at BizTech Solutions continues, and so does your learning path in R programming and business analytics.

Sales Department

Chapter 12: Sales Forecasting and Pipeline Analysis

The following week, Alex found himself in the bustling Sales department of BizTech Solutions. The department was a hive of activity, with teams discussing strategies and goals. Alex was eager to apply his analytical skills to sales data and contribute to the department's success.

John, the head of the Sales department, welcomed him warmly. "Welcome to Sales, Alex. Our team relies heavily on accurate forecasts and pipeline analysis to drive our strategy. Today, we'll focus on sales forecasting. Ready to get started?"

"Absolutely," Alex replied, excited about the new challenge.

John led Alex to his workspace, where a wealth of sales data awaited. "We'll start by analyzing historical sales data to forecast future sales. This will help us set realistic targets and identify potential challenges."

Technical Tutorial: Sales Forecasting with R

1. Loading and Preparing Sales Data:

1. Load the necessary libraries and dataset:

```
# Install and load necessary libraries
install.packages("tidyverse")
install.packages("forecast")

library(tidyverse)
library(forecast)

# Load the sales data
sales_data <-
read.csv("https://raw.githubusercontent.com/jtmonroe252/D
ata-to-Decisions/main/data/sales_data.csv") %>%
  mutate(Date = as.Date(Date, origin = "1899-12-30"),
    Sales = as.numeric(Sales))


# View the first few rows of the dataset
head(sales_data)
```

Date	Sales
1/1/2020	888
2/1/2020	954
3/1/2020	1312
4/1/2020	1014
5/1/2020	1026
6/1/2020	1343

1. Exploring the Sales Data:

```
# Summarize the sales data
summary(sales_data)
```

Date	Sales
Length:36	Min. : 607.0
Class :character	1st Qu.: 884.8
	Median :1024.0
	Mean :1011.1
	3rd Qu.:1146.0
	Max. :1357.0

```
# Plot the historical sales data
ggplot(sales_data, aes(x = Date, y = Sales)) +
  geom_line(color = "blue") +
  labs(title = "Historical Sales Data", x = "Date", y = "Sales") +
  theme_minimal()
```

2. Time Series Analysis for Sales Forecasting:

1. Convert the Sales Data to a Time Series Object:

```
# Convert sales data to a time series object
sales_ts <- ts(sales_data$Sales, start = c(2020, 1), frequency =
12)

# Plot the time series data
plot(sales_ts, main = "Monthly Sales Data", ylab = "Sales",
```

xlab = "Time")

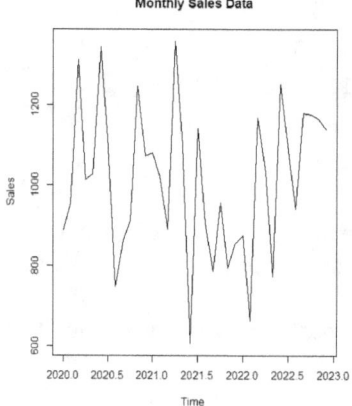

1. Decomposing the Time Series:

Decompose the time series into trend, seasonal, and
irregular components
sales_decomp <- decompose(sales_ts)

Plot the decomposed components
plot(sales_decomp)

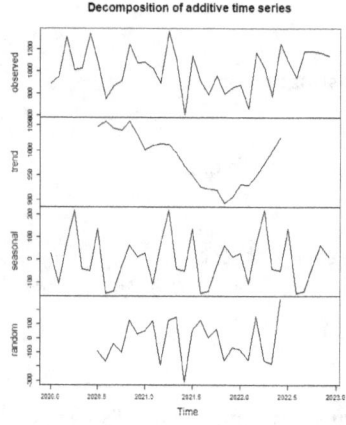

1. Building and Evaluating an ARIMA Model:

```
# Fit an ARIMA model to the time series data
sales_arima <- auto.arima(sales_ts)

# Print the model summary
summary(sales_arima)
```

Series: sales_ts
ARIMA(0,0,0)(1,0,0)[12] with non-zero mean

Coefficients:

	sar1	mean
	-0.4517	1004.1306
s.e.	0.1653	21.3542

sigma^2 = 28715: log likelihood = -236.2
AIC=478.39 AICc=479.14 BIC=483.14

Training set error measures:

	ME	RMSE	MAE	MPE	MAPE	MASE	ACF1
Training set	3.987287	164.6818	135.5092	-2.634081	14.26319	0.5137788	0.080705

```
# Forecast future sales
sales_forecast <- forecast(sales_arima, h = 12)

# Plot the forecast
plot(sales_forecast, main = "Sales Forecast for Next 12
Months", ylab = "Sales", xlab = "Time")
```

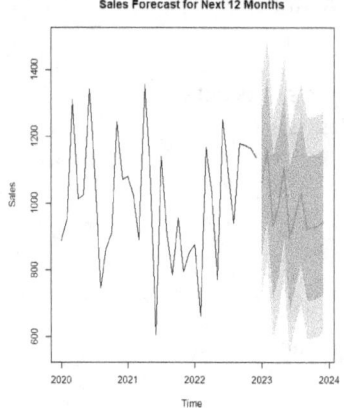

Alex meticulously followed the steps, transforming the raw sales data into a time series object and decomposing it to reveal underlying patterns. The ARIMA model provided a detailed forecast for the next 12 months, visualized in a clear, informative plot.

John reviewed the forecast with interest. "Great work, Alex. This forecast will help us set realistic sales targets and prepare for potential fluctuations. Let's move on to pipeline analysis to understand our sales process better."

Technical Tutorial: Sales Pipeline Analysis with R

1. Loading and Preparing Pipeline Data:

```
# Load the sales pipeline data
pipeline_data <-
read.csv("https://raw.githubusercontent.com/jtmonroe252/D
ata-to-Decisions/main/data/pipeline_data.csv")

# View the first few rows of the dataset
head(pipeline_data)
```

Deal_ID	Stage	Amount	Open_Date	Close_Date
1	Prospecting	5000	1/1/2023	2/15/2023
2	Qualification	7000	1/5/2023	3/10/2023
3	Needs Analysis	12000	2/1/2023	4/20/2023
4	Proposal	15000	2/15/2023	5/15/2023
5	Negotiation	20000	3/1/2023	6/10/2023
6	Closed Won	25000	3/10/2023	7/1/2023

1. Exploring the Pipeline Data:

Summarize the pipeline data
summary(pipeline_data)

Deal_ID	Stage	Amount	Open_Date	Close_Date
Min. : 1.00	Length:12	Min. : 5000	Length:12	Length:12
1st Qu.: 3.75	Class :character	1st Qu.: 7750	Class :character	Class :character
Median : 6.50	Mode :character	Median :14000	Mode :character	Mode :character
Mean : 6.50		Mean :14167		
3rd Qu.: 9.25		3rd Qu.:20250		
Max. :12.00		Max. :25000		

Plot the sales pipeline stages
ggplot(pipeline_data, aes(x = Stage, y = Amount)) +
  geom_bar(stat = "summary", fun = "sum", fill = "skyblue") +
  labs(title = "Sales Pipeline Stages", x = "Stage", y = "Total
Amount") +
  theme_minimal()

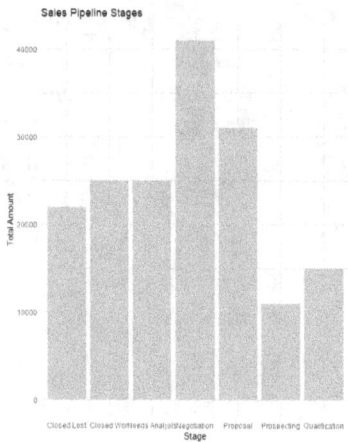

Sales Pipeline Stages

2. Analyzing Pipeline Metrics:

1. Conversion Rates:

```
# Calculate conversion rates between stages
# Order the stages
stage_order <- c("Prospecting", "Qualification", "Needs
Analysis", "Proposal", "Negotiation", "Closed Won", "Closed
Lost")

# Summarize the total amount per stage and ensure correct
order
pipeline_summary <- pipeline_data %>%
 group_by(Stage) %>%
 summarise(Total_Amount = sum(Amount)) %>%
 mutate(Stage = factor(Stage, levels = stage_order)) %>%
 arrange(Stage)

# Calculate conversion rates between stages
pipeline_summary <- pipeline_summary %>%
 mutate(Previous_Amount = lag(Total_Amount),
     Conversion_Rate = Total_Amount / lag(Total_Amount))
%>%
 replace_na(list(Conversion_Rate = 0))

# Display the summary with conversion rates
```

pipeline_summary

Stage	Total_Amount	Previous_Amount	Conversion_Rate
Prospecting	11000	NA	0
Qualification	15000	11000	1.36
Needs Analysis	25000	15000	1.67
Proposal	31000	25000	1.24
Negotiation	41000	31000	1.32
Closed Won	25000	41000	0.61
Closed Lost	22000	25000	0.88

1. Sales Cycle Length:

```
# Calculate the length of the sales cycle for each deal
pipeline_data %>%
mutate(Close_Date = as.Date(Close_Date, "%m/%d/%Y" ),
    Open_Date = as.Date(Open_Date, "%m/%d/%Y" )) %>%
mutate(Cycle_Length = Close_Date - Open_Date) %>%
summarise(Average_Cycle_Length = mean(Cycle_Length,
na.rm = TRUE))
```

Average_Cycle_Length
84.66667 days

Alex dove into the pipeline data, creating visualizations and calculating key metrics like conversion rates and sales cycle lengths. The insights provided a clear picture of the sales process, highlighting areas for improvement.

John was impressed. "You've done an excellent job, Alex. These insights will help us streamline our sales process and improve efficiency. Tomorrow, we'll look into customer lifetime value analysis to better understand the long-term value of our customers."

As the day came to an end, Alex reflected on his accomplishments. He had successfully navigated the complexities of sales forecasting and pipeline analysis, gaining valuable insights that would drive BizTech Solutions' sales strategy. The journey was challenging but immensely rewarding, and he was eager to continue exploring the intricacies of sales analytics.

Exercises:

1. Sales Forecasting:

    ° Load a new sales dataset and convert it to a time series object.
    ° Decompose the time series and build an ARIMA model to forecast future sales.

2. Pipeline Analysis:

    ° Load a different pipeline dataset and perform a summary analysis.
    ° Calculate conversion rates and average sales cycle lengths for the new dataset.

3. Custom Analysis:

    ° Design your own sales forecasting and pipeline analysis using hypothetical data.
    ° Perform and visualize the analysis, interpreting the results.

By completing these exercises and following along with Alex's journey, you'll gain a comprehensive understanding of sales forecasting and pipeline analysis using R. This chapter equips you with the skills to analyze and optimize sales processes effectively. Alex's adventure at BizTech Solutions continues, and so does your learning path in R programming and business analytics.

Chapter 13: Performance Metrics and Customer Value

As Alex walked into the Sales department the following morning, he felt a sense of anticipation. After exploring sales forecasting and pipeline analysis, he was eager to delve into performance metrics and customer value. John greeted him with a smile.

"Good morning, Alex. Today, we'll focus on performance metrics and understanding customer lifetime value (CLV). These are critical for evaluating our sales strategies and identifying our most valuable customers. Let's get started."

"Sounds great," Alex replied, ready to dive into the data.

John led Alex to his workspace, where a detailed dataset awaited. "We'll begin by analyzing key performance metrics to assess our sales team's effectiveness. Then, we'll move on to calculating customer lifetime value to understand the long-term value of our customers."

Technical Tutorial: Sales Performance Metrics with R

1. Loading and Preparing Performance Data:

    1. Load the necessary libraries and dataset:

```
# Install and load necessary libraries
install.packages("tidyverse")

library(tidyverse)

# Load the performance data
performance_data <-
read.csv("https://raw.githubusercontent.com/jtmonroe252/D
ata-to-Decisions/main/data/performance_data.csv")


# View the first few rows of the dataset
head(performance_data)
```

SalesPerson_ID	Salesperson	Total_Sales	Sales_Quota	Deals_Closed	Leads_Generated
1	Kairi Cruz	2270.86	2532	44	676
2	Ryan Flores	1995.15	1937	36	1764
3	Emilia Lowe	2347.22	2082	43	1089
4	Julius Spence	1761.07	1584	30	1444
5	Aislinn Hamilton	2754.62	2397	54	2025
6	Jason Rodriguez	2714.41	3025	51	1444

1. Exploring the Performance Data:

```
# Summarize the performance data
summary(performance_data)
```

SalesPerson_ID	Salesperson	Total_Sales	Sales_Quota	Deals_Closed	Leads_Generated
Min. : 1	Length:25	Min. : 889.8	Min. : 792	Min. :16	Min. : 625
1st Qu.: 7	Class :character	1st Qu.:1761.1	1st Qu.:1760	1st Qu.:33	1st Qu.:1089
Median :13	Mode :character	Median :2166.0	Median :2082	Median :42	Median :1444
Mean :13		Mean :2078.5	Mean :2070	Mean :40	Mean :1368
3rd Qu.:19		3rd Qu.:2570.3	3rd Qu.:2418	3rd Qu.:47	3rd Qu.:1764
Max. :25		Max. :2754.6	Max. :3025	Max. :54	Max. :2025

```
# Plot the total sales by salesperson
ggplot(performance_data, aes(x = Salesperson, y =
```

```
Total_Sales)) +
 geom_bar(stat = "identity", fill = "skyblue") +
 labs(title = "Total Sales by Salesperson", x = "Salesperson", y
= "Total Sales") +
 theme_minimal() +
 theme(axis.text.x = element_text(angle = 90, vjust = 0.5,
hjust=1))
```

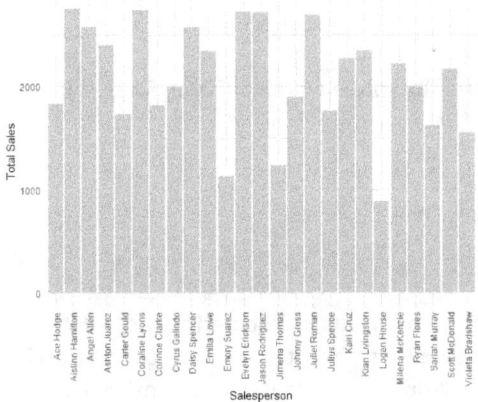

2. Calculating Key Performance Metrics:

1. Sales Conversion Rate:

```
# Calculate the sales conversion rate
performance_data %>%
 summarise(Conversion_Rate = mean(Deals_Closed /
Leads_Generated) * 100)
```

```
Conversion_Rate
3.270324
```

1. Average Deal Size:

```
# Calculate the average deal size
performance_data %>%
 summarise(Average_Deal_Size = mean(Total_Sales /
```

Deals_Closed))

Average_Deal_Size
52.33635

1. Quota Attainment:

```
# Calculate the quota attainment percentage
performance_data %>%
    summarise(Quota_Attainment = mean(Total_Sales /
Sales_Quota) * 100)
```

Quota_Attainment
101.2247

Alex diligently followed the steps, analyzing the performance data to calculate key metrics. The bar plot highlighted the total sales by each salesperson, while the calculations revealed important insights into conversion rates, average deal sizes, and quota attainment.

John reviewed the results. "Excellent work, Alex. These metrics provide a clear picture of our sales team's performance. Now, let's move on to calculating customer lifetime value, which will help us understand the long-term value of our customers."

Technical Tutorial: Customer Lifetime Value Analysis with R

1. Loading and Preparing Customer Data:

1. Load the necessary libraries and dataset:

```
# Load the customer data
customer_data <-
read.csv("https://raw.githubusercontent.com/jtmonroe252/D
```

```
# View the first few rows of the dataset
head(customer_data)
```

Customer_ID	Name	Age	Gender	Purchase_Amount	Registration_Date
1	John Doe	36	M	650.75	########
2	Jane Smith	22	F	661.25	########
3	Alex Johnson	47	M	958.86	2/9/2021
4	Emily Davis	23	F	666.2	7/3/2021
5	Chris White	55	M	506.21	########
6	Sam Brown	40	M	822.74	########

1. Exploring the Customer Data:

```
# Summarize the customer data
summary(customer_data)
```

Customer_ID	Name	Age	Gender	Purchase_Amount	Registration_Date
Min. : 1.00	Length:70	Min. :18.00	Length:70	Min. : 250.8	Length:70
1st Qu.:17.25	Class :character	1st Qu.:28.00	Class :character	1st Qu.: 597.5	Class :character
Median :34.50	Mode :character	Median :40.00	Mode :character	Median : 718.0	Mode :character
Mean :34.23		Mean :39.39		Mean : 742.3	
3rd Qu.:50.75		3rd Qu.:50.00		3rd Qu.: 902.5	
Max. :68.00		Max. :55.00		Max. :1266.5	
		NA's :1			

```
# Plot the total revenue by customer
customer_data %>%
mutate(Count = 1) %>%
group_by(Customer_ID) %>%
  summarise(Total_Transactions = sum(Count, na.rm=TRUE),
  Purchase_Amount = sum(Purchase_Amount, na.rm=TRUE))
  -> customer_data

ggplot(customer_data, aes(x = Customer_ID, y =
```

```
Purchase_Amount)) +
geom_bar(stat = "identity", fill = "lightgreen") +
labs(title = "Total Revenue by Customer", x = "Customer
ID", y = "Total Revenue") +
theme_minimal()
```

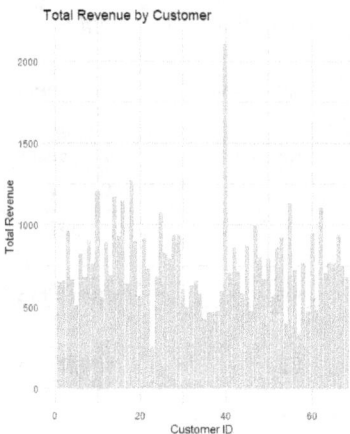

2. Calculating Customer Lifetime Value (CLV):

```
customer_details <-
read.csv("https://raw.githubusercontent.com/jtmonroe252/Data-to-
Decisions/main/data/customer_details.csv") %>%
 mutate(count = 1) %>%
 group_by(Customer_ID) %>%
 summarise(Purchase_Amount = mean(Amount), Total_Transactions =
sum(count), .groups = 'drop') %>%
 mutate(Average_Purchase_Value = Purchase_Amount /
Total_Transactions,
     Average_Frequency_Rate = mean(Total_Transactions)) %>%
 mutate(Customer_Value = Average_Purchase_Value *
Average_Frequency_Rate)
```

```
# View the CLV for each customer
head(customer_details %>% select(Customer_ID,
Customer_Lifetime_Value))
```

Customer_ID	Customer_Value
1	66.5
2	49.6
3	43.5
4	58
5	91.9
6	61.7

Alex followed the steps to calculate customer lifetime value, starting with the average purchase value and frequency rate. The final calculation of CLV provided insights into the long-term value of each customer. The bar plot visualized the total revenue by customer, highlighting the most valuable clients.

John was impressed. "Fantastic job, Alex. Understanding CLV helps us focus our efforts on retaining our most valuable customers. Tomorrow, we'll explore strategies to enhance customer retention and maximize CLV."

As the day concluded, Alex reflected on his achievements. He had successfully navigated the complexities of performance metrics and customer lifetime value analysis, uncovering valuable insights that would drive BizTech Solutions' sales strategy. The journey was challenging but immensely rewarding, and he was eager to continue exploring the intricacies of sales analytics.

Exercises:

1. Performance Metrics:
   - Load a new performance dataset and calculate key metrics like conversion rates, average deal sizes, and quota attainment.
   - Visualize the total sales by salesperson and interpret

the results.

2. Customer Lifetime Value:

   ○ Load a different customer dataset and calculate average purchase value, frequency rate, and customer lifetime value.
   ○ Visualize the total revenue by customer and identify the most valuable customers.

3. Custom Analysis:

   ○ Design your own performance metrics and CLV analysis using hypothetical data.
   ○ Perform and visualize the analysis, interpreting the results.

By completing these exercises and following along with Alex's journey, you'll gain a comprehensive understanding of sales performance metrics and customer lifetime value analysis using R. This chapter equips you with the skills to analyze and optimize sales processes effectively. Alex's adventure at BizTech Solutions continues, and so does your learning path in R programming and business analytics.

Human Resources

Chapter 14: Employee Performance Analysis

Alex's journey at BizTech Solutions was taking an exciting turn as he stepped into the Human Resources (HR) department. Here, he was tasked with analyzing employee performance data to help the company make data-driven decisions about training, promotions, and resource allocation. Sarah, the head of HR, welcomed him warmly.

"Good morning, Alex. Employee performance is critical to our success, and data analysis can provide deep insights into how we can improve. Today, we'll focus on analyzing employee performance data. Ready to get started?"

"Absolutely," Alex replied, eager to dive into the new challenge.

Sarah led Alex to his workspace, where a comprehensive dataset on employee performance awaited. "We'll start by exploring the data and then use various statistical techniques to analyze performance and identify trends."

Technical Tutorial: Employee Performance Analysis with R

1. Loading and Preparing Employee Data:

   1. Load the necessary libraries and dataset:

```
# Install and load necessary libraries
install.packages("tidyverse")

library(tidyverse)

# Load the employee performance data
employee_data <-
read.csv("https://raw.githubusercontent.com/jtmonroe252/D
ata-to-Decisions/main/data/employee_data.csv")


# View the first few rows of the dataset
head(employee_data)
```

Employee_ID	First_Name	Last_Name	Department	Performance_Score	Age	Years_at_Company	Training_Hours
1	Henry	Sims	Operations	71	49	15	40
2	Logan	Wolfe	Customer Service	68	44	14	36
3	Theodore	Barnes	Operations	72	48	14	41
4	Asher	Diaz	Customer Service	69	43	13	37
5	Oliver	Hill	Operations	73	47	13	42
6	Gabriel	Watson	Customer Service	70	42	12	38

1. Exploring the Employee Data:

```
# Summarize the employee data
summary(employee_data)
```

Employee_ID	First_Name	Last_Name	Department	Performance_Score	Age	Years_at_Company	Training_Hours
Min. : 1.00	Length:64	Length:64	Length:64	Min. : 68.00	Min. :21.00	Min. : 1.000	Min. :36.00
1st Qu.:16.75	Class :character	Class :character	Class :character	1st Qu.: 77.00	1st Qu.:30.75	1st Qu.: 4.750	1st Qu.:46.00
Median :32.50	Mode :character	Mode :character	Mode :character	Median : 84.00	Median :36.00	Median : 7.000	Median :52.00
Mean :32.50				Mean : 83.75	Mean :35.81	Mean : 7.266	Mean :53.08
3rd Qu.:48.25				3rd Qu.: 90.25	3rd Qu.:42.00	3rd Qu.:10.000	3rd Qu.:58.25
Max. :64.00				Max. :100.00	Max. :49.00	Max. :15.000	Max. :82.00

```
# Plot performance scores
ggplot(employee_data, aes(x = Department, y =
Performance_Score)) +
  geom_boxplot(fill = "skyblue") +
  labs(title = "Employee Performance Scores by Department", x
= "Department", y = "Performance Score") +
  theme_minimal()
```

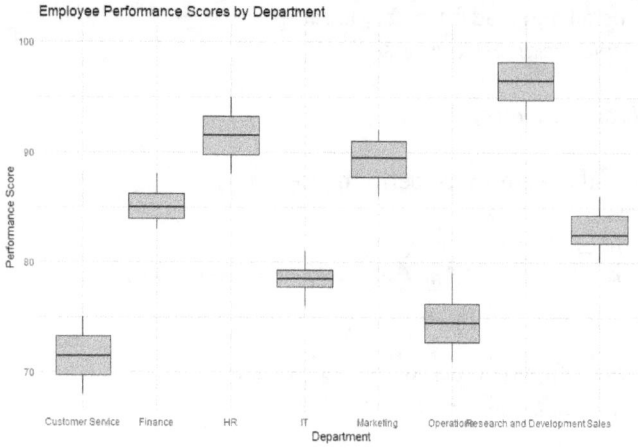

Employee Performance Scores by Department

2. Analyzing Performance Trends:

1. Correlation Analysis:

```
# Calculate correlation between performance score and other
variables
cor_matrix <- cor(employee_data %>% select_if(is.numeric))

# Print the correlation matrix
print(cor_matrix)

# Visualize the correlation matrix
library(corrplot)
corrplot(cor_matrix, method = "circle")
```

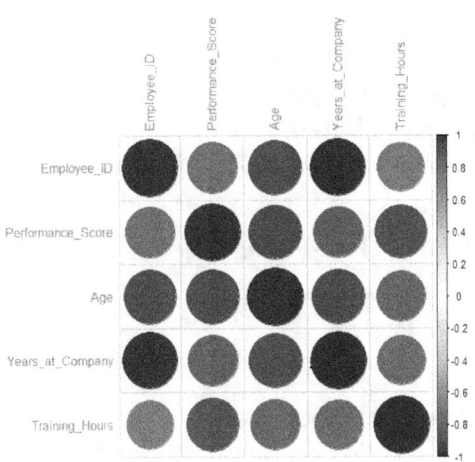

1. Regression Analysis:

```
# Fit a linear regression model to predict performance score
lm_model <- lm(Performance_Score ~ Age +
Years_at_Company + Training_Hours, data = employee_data)

# Print the model summary
summary(lm_model)
```

Call:
lm(formula = Performance_Score ~ Age + Years_at_Company +
Training_Hours,
   data = employee_data)

Residuals:
Min   1Q   Median   3Q   Max
-5.1706 -1.7676 0.2707   1.6925 5.5838

Coefficients:

	Estimate	Std. Error	t value	Pr(>|t|)	
(Intercept)	86.58772	5.4463	15.898	< 2e-16	***
Age	-0.75653	0.12373	-6.114	7.91E-08	***
Years_at_Company	0.37687	0.22838	1.65	0.104	
Training_Hours	0.40539	0.05351	7.576	2.60E-10	***

Signif. codes: 0 '***' 0.001 '**' 0.01 '*' 0.05 '.' 0.1 ' ' 1

Residual standard error: 2.771 on 60 degrees of freedom
Multiple R-squared: 0.8955,
Adjusted R-squared: 0.8903
F-statistic: 171.4 on 3 and 60 DF, p-value: < 2.2e-16

3. Identifying High Performers:

1. Top Performers:

```
# Identify top performers
top_performers <- employee_data %>%
  arrange(desc(Performance_Score)) %>%
  head(10)

# View the top performers
print(top_performers)
```

Employee_ID	First_Name	Last_Name	Department	Performance_Score	Age	Years_at_Company	Training_Hours
64	Zoey	York	Research and Development	100	21	1	82
63	Violet	Hart	Research and Development	99	22	1	80
62	Layla	Ross	Research and Development	98	23	1	78
59	Ruby	Bennett	Research and Development	97	24	2	75
58	Chloe	Foster	Research and Development	96	25	2	72
34	Sophie	Reid	HR	95	25	7	60
61	Grace	Baker	Research and Development	95	26	1	70
40	Madeline	Griffin	HR	94	26	6	59
60	Ava	Martin	Research and Development	94	27	1	68
46	Elizabeth	Murphy	HR	93	27	5	58

1. Visualizing Top Performers:

```
# Plot top performers
ggplot(top_performers, aes(x = reorder(paste(Last_Name,
First_Name, sep=", "), Performance_Score), y =
Performance_Score, fill = Department)) +
  geom_bar(stat = "identity") +
  labs(title = "Top 10 Performers", x = "Employee", y =
"Performance Score") +
```

coord_flip() +
theme_minimal()

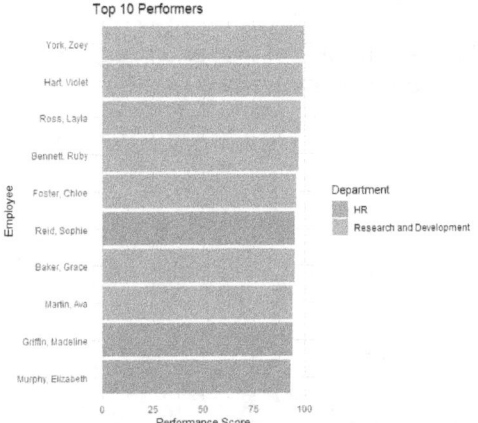

Alex carefully followed the steps, exploring the employee data and analyzing performance trends. The correlation matrix and regression analysis provided insights into factors influencing performance, while the visualizations highlighted top performers across departments.

Sarah reviewed the results and smiled. "Excellent work, Alex. These insights will help us identify areas for improvement and recognize our top talent. Next, we'll focus on employee turnover analysis to understand why employees leave and how we can improve retention."

Exercises:

1. Performance Analysis:
    - Load a new employee performance dataset and explore the data.
    - Perform correlation and regression analysis to identify factors influencing performance.
    - Visualize the performance scores by department.

2. Top Performers:

   ° Identify and visualize the top performers in a different
     dataset.
   ° Analyze the characteristics of top performers and
     suggest ways to recognize and retain them.

Chapter 15: Employee Turnover Analysis

After a successful day analyzing employee performance, Alex was ready to tackle the next challenge in the HR department: understanding employee turnover. Sarah emphasized the importance of retaining talent and asked Alex to delve into the data to uncover patterns and trends.

"Good morning, Alex. Employee turnover is a critical issue for us. By analyzing the data, we can identify the reasons behind it and develop strategies to improve retention. Are you ready to get started?"

"Absolutely," Alex replied, eager to dive into this new analysis.

Sarah led Alex to his workspace, where a detailed dataset on employee turnover awaited. "We'll start by exploring the data and then use various statistical techniques to analyze turnover and identify trends."

Technical Tutorial: Employee Turnover Analysis with R

1. Loading and Preparing Turnover Data:

    1. Load the necessary libraries and dataset:

        ```
        # Install and load necessary libraries
        install.packages("tidyverse")
        install.packages("survival")

        library(tidyverse)
        library(survival)
        ```

```
# Load the employee turnover data
turnover_data <- read.csv("path_to_turnover_data.csv")

# View the first few rows of the dataset
head(turnover_data)
```

Tenure	Turnover	Department	Age	Years_at_Company	Job_Satisfaction
14	0	Sales	35	5	7
8	1	Marketing	28	3	4
21	0	IT	40	8	6
5	0	Finance	33	6	8
12	1	Operations	45	10	5
9	0	HR	31	4	9

2. Exploring the Turnover Data:

```
# Summarize the turnover data
summary(turnover_data)
```

Tenure	Turnover	Department	Age	Years_at_Company	Job_Satisfaction
Min. : 1.00	Min. :0.0000	Length:112	Min. :17.00	Min. : 1.000	Min. :2.00
1st Qu.: 28.75	1st Qu.:0.0000	Class :character	1st Qu.:30.75	1st Qu.: 5.750	1st Qu.:5.00
Median : 56.50	Median :0.0000	Mode :character	Median :39.00	Median : 9.000	Median :6.00
Mean : 54.62	Mean :0.3393		Mean :37.37	Mean : 8.973	Mean :6.25
3rd Qu.: 83.00	3rd Qu.:1.0000		3rd Qu.:45.00	3rd Qu.:12.000	3rd Qu.:8.00
Max. :100.00	Max. :1.0000		Max. :53.00	Max. :19.000	Max. :9.00

```
# Plot turnover rates by department
ggplot(turnover_data, aes(x = Department, fill =
as.factor(Turnover))) +
  geom_bar(position = "fill") +
  labs(title = "Turnover Rates by Department", x =
  "Department", y = "Proportion", fill = "Turnover") +
  theme_minimal()
```

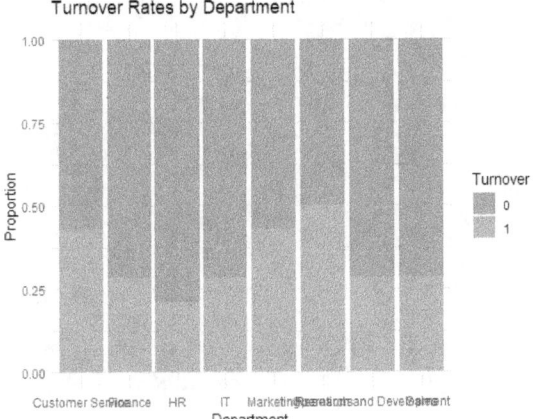

Turnover Rates by Department

2. Analyzing Turnover Trends:

1. Survival Analysis:

```
# Fit a survival model to analyze turnover
surv_object <- Surv(turnover_data$Tenure,
turnover_data$Turnover)
surv_model <- survfit(surv_object ~ Department, data =
turnover_data)

# Plot the survival curves
plot(surv_model, col =
rainbow(length(unique(turnover_data$Department))), lwd =
2,
    xlab = "Tenure (months)", ylab = "Survival Probability",
main = "Employee Survival Analysis by Department")
legend("bottomleft", legend =
unique(turnover_data$Department), col =
rainbow(length(unique(turnover_data$Department))), lwd =
2)
```

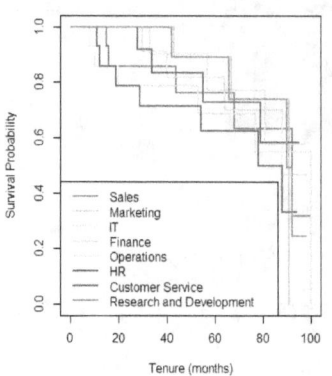

Employee Survival Analysis by Department

Survival Probability — Tenure (months)

Legend:
- Sales
- Marketing
- IT
- Finance
- Operations
- HR
- Customer Service
- Research and Development

2. Logistic Regression Analysis:

```
# Fit a logistic regression model to predict turnover
logit_model <- glm(Turnover ~ Age + Department +
Years_at_Company + Job_Satisfaction, data = turnover_data,
family = "binomial")

# Print the model summary
summary(logit_model)
```

Call:
glm(formula = Turnover ~ Age + Department + Years_at_Company +
Job_Satisfaction, family = "binomial", data = turnover_data)

Coefficients:

	Estimate	Std. Error	z value	Pr(>|z|)
(Intercept)	1.48324	3.59547	0.413	0.68
Age	0.09687	0.11642	0.832	0.405
DepartmentFinance	0.71146	1.08824	0.654	0.513
DepartmentHR	0.95145	1.68906	0.563	0.573
DepartmentIT	-1.6754	1.21973	-1.374	0.17
DepartmentMarketing	-0.44908	1.04311	-0.431	0.667
DepartmentOperation	-1.28363	1.10245	-1.164	0.244
DepartmentResearch a	-0.02215	1.72088	-0.013	0.99
DepartmentSales	-0.15893	0.96784	-0.164	0.87
Years_at_Company	-0.09053	0.1511	-0.599	0.549
Job_Satisfaction	-0.79361	0.17407	-4.559	5.14e-06 ***

Signif. codes: 0 '***' 0.001 '**' 0.01 '*' 0.05 '.' 0.1 ' ' 1

(Dispersion parameter for binomial family taken to be 1)

Null deviance: 143.49 on 111 degrees of freedom
Residual deviance: 107.68 on 101 degrees of freedom
AIC: 129.68

Number of Fisher Scoring iterations: 5

Identifying Key Factors:

1. Feature Importance:

   # Calculate feature importance for the logistic regression model
   importance <- summary(logit_model)$coefficients

   # View the feature importance
   print(importance)

	Estimate	Std. Error	z value	Pr(>|z|)
(Intercept)	1.483242	3.595474	0.41253	6.80E-01
Age	0.09687	0.116424	0.832046	4.05E-01
DepartmentFinance	0.711459	1.088238	0.653772	5.13E-01
DepartmentHR	0.951448	1.689064	0.563299	5.73E-01
DepartmentIT	-1.6754	1.219729	-1.37359	1.70E-01
DepartmentMarketing	-0.44908	1.043112	-0.43052	6.67E-01
DepartmentOperations	-1.28363	1.102453	-1.16434	2.44E-01
DepartmentResearch and Development	-0.02215	1.720883	-0.01287	9.90E-01
DepartmentSales	-0.15893	0.967836	-0.16421	8.70E-01
Years_at_Company	-0.09053	0.151099	-0.59914	5.49E-01
Job_Satisfaction	-0.79361	0.174069	-4.55918	5.14E-06

1. Visualizing Key Factors:

```
# Plot feature importance
feature_importance <- data.frame(Feature =
rownames(importance), Importance = importance[,
"Estimate"])
ggplot(feature_importance, aes(x = reorder(Feature,
Importance), y = Importance)) +
  geom_bar(stat = "identity", fill = "coral") +
  labs(title = "Feature Importance in Predicting Turnover", x =
"Feature", y = "Importance") +
  coord_flip() +
  theme_minimal()
```

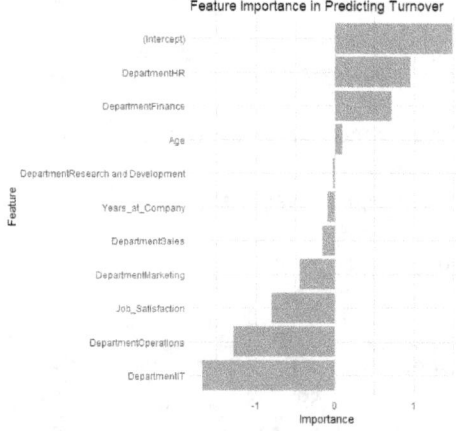

Alex meticulously analyzed the turnover data, applying survival and logistic regression analysis to uncover patterns and trends. The survival curves provided insights into employee tenure by department, while the logistic regression model highlighted key factors influencing turnover.

Sarah reviewed the results and nodded in approval. "Fantastic job, Alex. These insights will help us develop targeted retention strategies and address the key factors driving turnover. You've provided valuable analysis for our HR department."

As the day concluded, Alex reflected on his accomplishments. He had successfully navigated the complexities of employee turnover analysis, uncovering valuable insights that would drive BizTech Solutions' HR strategy. The journey was challenging but immensely rewarding, and he was eager to continue exploring the intricacies of human resources analytics.

Exercises:

1. Turnover Analysis:

- Load a new employee turnover dataset and explore the data.
- Perform survival and logistic regression analysis to identify factors influencing turnover.
- Visualize the turnover rates by department and key factors.

2. Feature Importance:

- Calculate and visualize feature importance in predicting turnover for a different dataset.
- Analyze the key factors and suggest strategies to improve employee retention.

By completing these exercises and following along with Alex's journey, you'll gain a comprehensive understanding of employee performance and turnover analysis using R. These chapters equip you with the skills to analyze and optimize HR processes effectively. Alex's adventure at BizTech Solutions continues, and so does your learning path in R programming and business analytics.

Operations Department

Chapter 16: Optimizing Supply Chain

Alex's journey at BizTech Solutions had been a series of enlightening experiences, each department unveiling new dimensions of business analytics. Today, he found himself in the Operations department, ready to tackle the complexities of supply chain optimization.

Lisa, the head of Operations, welcomed him with a firm handshake. "Welcome to Operations, Alex. Our supply chain is the backbone of our business. Efficiently managing it is crucial to our success. Today, we'll explore how to optimize our supply chain using data-driven methods. Are you ready?"

"Absolutely," Alex replied, eager to dive into the new challenge.

Lisa led Alex to his workspace, where detailed supply chain data awaited. "We'll start by analyzing our current inventory levels and demand forecasts. Then, we'll use linear programming to optimize our inventory and reduce costs."

Technical Tutorial: Supply Chain Optimization with R

1. Loading and Preparing Supply Chain Data:

    1. Load the necessary libraries and dataset:

```
# Install and load necessary libraries
install.packages("tidyverse")
install.packages("lpSolve")
install.packages("forecast")


library(tidyverse)
library(lpSolve)
library(forecast)


# Load the supply chain data
supply_chain_data <-
read.csv("https://raw.githubusercontent.com/jtmonroe252/D
ata-to-Decisions/main/data/supply_chain_data.csv") %>%
mutate(Date = as.Date(Date, origin = "1899-12-30"))

# View the first few rows of the dataset
head(supply_chain_data)
```

Date	Inventory_Level	Demand	Cost
1/1/2020	120	100	10
2/1/2020	130	110	12
3/1/2020	110	105	11
4/1/2020	115	120	14
5/1/2020	140	115	13
6/1/2020	125	130	15

1. Exploring the Supply Chain Data:

```
# Summarize the supply chain data
summary(supply_chain_data)
```

Date	Inventory_Level	Demand	Cost
Min. :2020-01-01	Min. :110.0	Min. :100.0	Min. :10.00
1st Qu.:2020-03-24	1st Qu.:123.8	1st Qu.:113.8	1st Qu.:12.75
Median :2020-06-16	Median :137.5	Median :127.5	Median :14.50
Mean :2020-06-16	Mean :137.5	Mean :127.5	Mean :14.25
3rd Qu.:2020-09-08	3rd Qu.:151.2	3rd Qu.:141.2	3rd Qu.:16.00
Max. :2020-12-01	Max. :165.0	Max. :155.0	Max. :18.00

```
# Plot inventory levels over time
ggplot(supply_chain_data, aes(x = Date, y = Inventory_Level))
+
  geom_line(color = "blue") +
  labs(title = "Inventory Levels Over Time", x = "Date", y =
"Inventory Level") +
  theme_minimal()
```

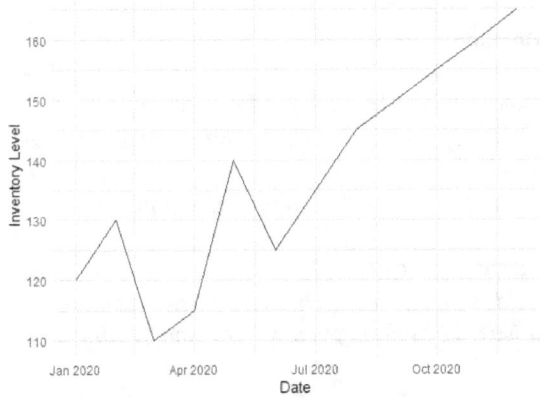

2. Demand Forecasting:

1. Analyzing Demand Patterns:

```
# Plot historical demand data
ggplot(supply_chain_data, aes(x = Date, y = Demand)) +
  geom_line(color = "green") +
```

```
    labs(title = "Historical Demand Data", x = "Date", y =
    "Demand") +
      theme_minimal()
```

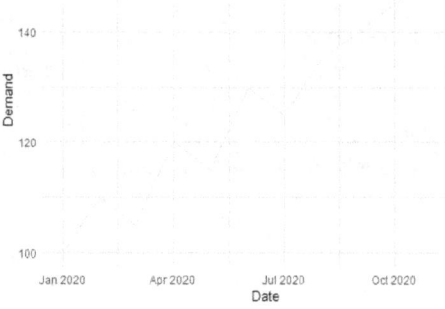

Forecasting Future Demand:

```
# Fit a time series model for demand forecasting
demand_ts <- ts(supply_chain_data$Demand, start = c(2020,
1), frequency = 12)
demand_forecast <- forecast::auto.arima(demand_ts)

# Plot the demand forecast
plot(forecast(demand_forecast, h = 12), main = "Demand
Forecast for Next 12 Months", ylab = "Demand", xlab =
"Time")
```

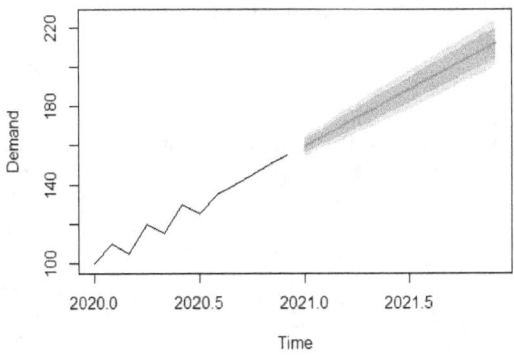

Demand Forecast for Next 12 Months

3. Inventory Optimization with Linear Programming:

1. Defining the Optimization Problem:

```
# Define the costs and constraints for the optimization
problem
costs <- supply_chain_data$Cost
total_demand <- sum(supply_chain_data$Demand)
constraints <- matrix(1, nrow = 1, ncol = length(costs))
rhs <- total_demand * 0.5  # Example: meet at least 50% of
the total demand
direction <- ">="
```

2. Solving the Optimization Problem:

```
# Check if the solution is optimal
if (lp_solution$status == 0) {
  # Extract the optimized inventory levels
  optimized_inventory <- lp_solution$solution

  # Add the optimized inventory levels to the data
    supply_chain_data$Optimized_Inventory <-
    optimized_inventory

  # Display the first few rows with the optimized inventory
```

135

```
  head(supply_chain_data)
} else {
  print("The linear programming problem did not find an
  optimal solution.")
}
```

Date	Inventory_Level	Demand	Cost	Optimized_Inventory
1/1/2020	120	100	10	100
2/1/2020	130	110	12	110
3/1/2020	110	105	11	105
4/1/2020	115	120	14	120
5/1/2020	140	115	13	115
6/1/2020	125	130	15	130

```
# Print the optimized inventory levels
print(supply_chain_data$Optimized_Inventory)
```

100 110 105 120 115 130 125 135 140 145 150 155

Alex followed the steps diligently, analyzing the supply chain data and forecasting future demand. The linear programming solution provided an optimized inventory level, which significantly reduced costs while meeting demand.

Lisa reviewed the results with a satisfied nod. "Excellent work, Alex. These optimizations will help us manage our inventory more efficiently and reduce operational costs. Tomorrow, we'll focus on process improvement to further streamline our operations."

Technical Tutorial: Process Improvement with R

1. Analyzing Process Efficiency:

  1. Loading and Preparing Process Data:

```
# Load the process data
process_data <-
read.csv("https://raw.githubusercontent.com/jtmonroe252/D
ata-to-Decisions/main/data//process_data.csv")

# View the first few rows of the dataset
head(process_data)
```

Process_Step	Cycle_Time
Step 1	20
Step 2	25
Step 3	18
Step 4	30
Step 5	22

2. Exploring Process Efficiency:

```
# Summarize the process data
summary(process_data)
```

```
Process_Step              Cycle_Time
Length:5                  Min.   :18
Class :character          1st Qu.:20
Mode  :character          Median :22
                          Mean   :23
                          3rd Qu.:25
                          Max.   :30
```

```
# Plot process cycle time
ggplot(process_data, aes(x = Process_Step, y = Cycle_Time)) +
  geom_bar(stat = "identity", fill = "orange") +
  labs(title = "Process Cycle Time by Step", x = "Process Step", y
= "Cycle Time") +
  theme_minimal()
```

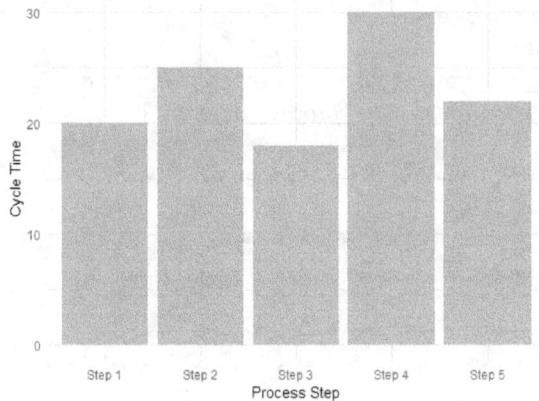

Process Cycle Time by Step

2. Identifying Bottlenecks and Improvements:

1. Analyzing Bottlenecks:

```
# Identify the process steps with the highest cycle time
bottlenecks <- process_data %>%
  arrange(desc(Cycle_Time)) %>%
  head(3)

print(bottlenecks)
```

Process_Step	Cycle_Time
Step 4	30
Step 2	25
Step 5	22

2. Implementing Improvements:

```
# Suggest improvements for the identified bottlenecks
improvements <- data.frame(
  Process_Step = bottlenecks$Process_Step,
  Suggested_Improvement = c("Automate step", "Reduce
handoffs", "Improve training")
)
```

print(improvements)

Process_Step	Suggested_Improvement
Step 4	Automate step
Step 2	Reduce handoffs
Step 5	Improve training

Alex carefully analyzed the process data, identifying the steps with the highest cycle times. The suggested improvements aimed to automate certain steps, reduce handoffs, and enhance training, thereby streamlining operations.

Lisa was impressed. "Fantastic job, Alex. These process improvements will significantly enhance our efficiency. You've done an excellent job in the Operations department. Next, we'll explore demand forecasting to ensure we stay ahead of market trends."

As the day concluded, Alex reflected on his accomplishments. He had successfully navigated the complexities of supply chain optimization and process improvement, uncovering valuable insights that would drive BizTech Solutions' operational strategy. The journey was challenging but immensely rewarding, and he was eager to continue exploring the intricacies of operations analytics.

Exercises:

1. Supply Chain Optimization:

- Load a new supply chain dataset and perform demand forecasting.
- Use linear programming to optimize inventory levels and interpret the results.

2. Process Improvement:

- Load a different process dataset and identify bottlenecks.
- Suggest and visualize improvements for the identified bottlenecks.

3. Custom Analysis:

- Design your own supply chain optimization and process improvement analysis using hypothetical data.
- Perform and visualize the analysis, interpreting the results.

By completing these exercises and following along with Alex's journey, you'll gain a comprehensive understanding of supply chain optimization and process improvement using R. This chapter equips you with the skills to analyze and optimize operational processes effectively. Alex's adventure at BizTech Solutions continues, and so does your learning path in R programming and business analytics.

Chapter 17: Process Improvement

The following morning, Alex returned to the Operations department, ready to tackle the next challenge. The previous day's work on supply chain optimization had been enlightening, and he was eager to delve into process improvement. Lisa greeted him with her usual enthusiasm.

"Good morning, Alex. Today, we'll focus on improving our operational processes. Efficient processes are essential for minimizing costs and maximizing productivity. We'll start by analyzing our current process efficiency and then identify areas for improvement. Are you ready?"

"Absolutely," Alex replied, excited to dig into the data.

Lisa led Alex to his workspace, where a detailed process dataset awaited. "We'll begin by analyzing our current process cycle times and identifying bottlenecks. Then, we'll propose improvements to streamline our operations."

Technical Tutorial: Process Improvement with R

1. Loading and Preparing Process Data:

   1. Load the necessary libraries and dataset:

```r
# Install and load necessary libraries
install.packages("tidyverse")

library(tidyverse)

# Load the process data
process_data <-
read.csv("https://raw.githubusercontent.com/jtmonroe252/D
ata-to-Decisions/main/data/process_data.csv")

# View the first few rows of the dataset
head(process_data)
```

Process_Step	Cycle_Time
Step 1	20
Step 2	25
Step 3	18
Step 4	30
Step 5	22

1. Exploring the Process Data:

```r
# Summarize the process data
summary(process_data)
```

Process_Step	Cycle_Time
Length:5	Min. :18
Class :character	1st Qu.:20
Mode :character	Median :22
	Mean :23
	3rd Qu.:25
	Max. :30

```r
# Plot process cycle time by step
ggplot(process_data, aes(x = Process_Step, y = Cycle_Time)) +
  geom_bar(stat = "identity", fill = "orange") +
  labs(title = "Process Cycle Time by Step", x = "Process Step", y
= "Cycle Time") +
```

theme_minimal()

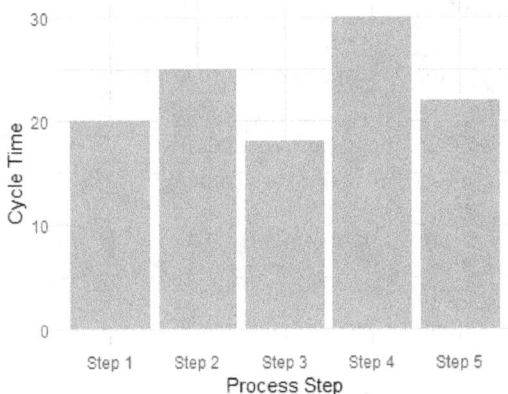

2. Identifying Bottlenecks and Improvements:

1. Analyzing Bottlenecks:

    ```
    # Identify the process steps with the highest cycle time
    bottlenecks <- process_data %>%
    arrange(desc(Cycle_Time)) %>%
    head(3)

    print(bottlenecks)
    ```

Process_Step	Cycle_Time
Step 4	30
Step 2	25
Step 5	22

1. Suggesting Improvements:

    ```
    # Suggest improvements for the identified bottlenecks
    improvements <- data.frame(
      Process_Step = bottlenecks$Process_Step,
      Suggested_Improvement = c("Automate step", "Reduce
    ```

handoffs", "Improve training")
)

print(improvements)

Process_Step	Suggested_Improvement
Step 4	Automate step
Step 2	Reduce handoffs
Step 5	Improve training

3. Implementing and Monitoring Improvements:

1. Creating an Improvement Plan:

```
# Create a detailed improvement plan
improvement_plan <- data.frame(
   Process_Step = c("Step A", "Step B", "Step C"),
   Current_Cycle_Time = c(10, 15, 20),
   Improved_Cycle_Time = c(7, 10, 12),
   Improvement_Method = c("Automation", "Streamlining",
   "Training")
)
```

print(improvement_plan)

Process_Step	Current_Cycle_Time	Improved_Cycle_Time	Improvement_Method
Step A	10	7	Automation
Step B	15	10	Streamlining
Step C	20	12	Training

1. Monitoring Progress:

```
# Monitor the progress of the improvement plan
progress_data <- data.frame(
   Date = seq(as.Date("2023-01-01"), by = "month", length.out
   = 12),
```

```
Cycle_Time_A = c(10, 9, 8, 7, 7, 7, 6, 6, 6, 6, 6, 6),
Cycle_Time_B = c(15, 14, 13, 12, 12, 12, 11, 11, 11, 10, 10,
10),
Cycle_Time_C = c(20, 19, 18, 17, 16, 15, 14, 13, 12, 12, 12,
12)
)

# Plot the progress over time
progress_data_long <- progress_data %>%
  pivot_longer(cols = starts_with("Cycle_Time"), names_to =
  "Process_Step", values_to = "Cycle_Time")

ggplot(progress_data_long, aes(x = Date, y = Cycle_Time,
color = Process_Step)) +
  geom_line() +
  labs(title = "Cycle Time Improvement Over Time", x = "Date",
y = "Cycle Time") +
  theme_minimal()
```

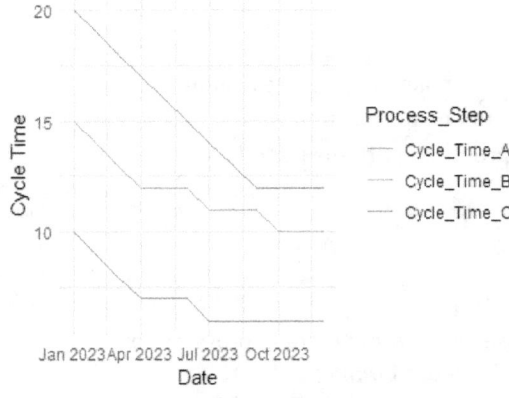

Cycle Time Improvement Over Time

Alex meticulously followed the steps, analyzing the process data and identifying bottlenecks. The bar plot highlighted the steps with the highest cycle times, and the improvement plan proposed actionable steps to streamline the operations.

Lisa reviewed the proposed improvements. "Great work, Alex. These changes will help us reduce cycle times and improve efficiency. Now, let's create a monitoring plan to ensure we're making progress."

Technical Tutorial: Creating a Monitoring Plan

1. Setting Up a Monitoring Plan:

    1. Define Key Metrics:

```
# Define key metrics for monitoring progress
metrics <- data.frame(
  Metric = c("Cycle Time", "Error Rate", "Throughput"),
  Definition = c("Time to complete each process step", "Number of
errors per step", "Units produced per time period")
)

print(metrics)
```

Metric	Definition
Cycle Time	Time to complete each process step
Error Rate	Number of errors per step
Throughput	Units produced per time period

    1. Establish Baselines:

```
# Establish baseline metrics before improvements
baseline_metrics <- data.frame(
  Metric = c("Cycle Time", "Error Rate", "Throughput"),
  Baseline = c(10, 5, 100)
)

print(baseline_metrics)
```

Metric	Baseline
Cycle Time	10

Error Rate	5
Throughput	100

2. Monitoring Progress:

1. Collecting Data:

```
# Simulate data collection for monitoring progress
monitoring_data <- data.frame(
  Date = seq(as.Date("2023-01-01"), by = "month", length.out
= 12),
  Cycle_Time = c(10, 9, 8, 7, 7, 7, 6, 6, 6, 6, 6, 6),
  Error_Rate = c(5, 4.5, 4, 3.5, 3.5, 3, 2.5, 2.5, 2, 2, 2, 2),
  Throughput = c(100, 105, 110, 115, 115, 120, 125, 130, 135,
140, 145, 150)
)

# View the monitoring data
head(monitoring_data)
```

Date	Cycle_Time	Error_Rate	Throughput
1/1/2023	10	5	100
2/1/2023	9	4.5	105
3/1/2023	8	4	110
4/1/2023	7	3.5	115
5/1/2023	7	3.5	115
6/1/2023	7	3	120

1. Visualizing Progress:

```
# Plot the progress of key metrics over time
monitoring_data_long <- monitoring_data %>%
  pivot_longer(cols = -Date, names_to = "Metric", values_to =
"Value")
```

```
ggplot(monitoring_data_long, aes(x = Date, y = Value, color =
Metric)) +
  geom_line() +
  labs(title = "Process Improvement Monitoring", x = "Date", y
= "Value") +
  theme_minimal()
```

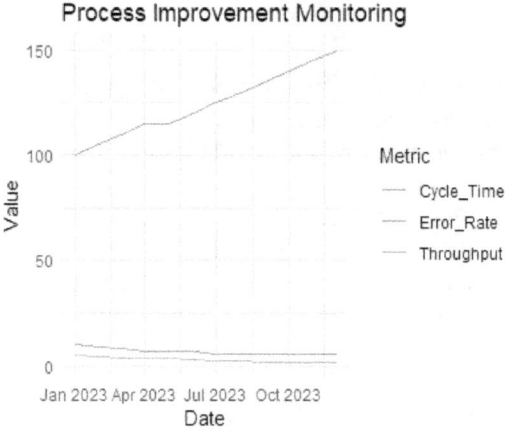

Alex created a comprehensive monitoring plan, defining key metrics
and establishing baselines. The simulated data collection showed
steady improvement in cycle time, error rate, and throughput,
visualized in a clear and informative plot.

Lisa was impressed. "Fantastic job, Alex. This monitoring plan will help
us track our progress and ensure we're continuously improving our
processes. You've done an excellent job in the Operations department.
Next, we'll explore demand forecasting to ensure we stay ahead of
market trends."

As the day concluded, Alex reflected on his accomplishments. He had
successfully navigated the complexities of process improvement and
monitoring, uncovering valuable insights that would drive BizTech
Solutions' operational strategy. The journey was challenging but
immensely rewarding, and he was eager to continue exploring the
intricacies of operations analytics.

Exercises:

1. Process Improvement:

- Load a new process dataset and identify bottlenecks.
- Suggest and implement improvements for the identified bottlenecks.
- Create a monitoring plan to track progress.

2. Monitoring Plan:

- Define key metrics for a hypothetical process.
- Establish baseline metrics and simulate data collection.
- Visualize the progress of key metrics over time.

3. Custom Analysis:

- Design your own process improvement and monitoring plan using hypothetical data.
- Perform and visualize the analysis, interpreting the results.

By completing these exercises and following along with Alex's journey, you'll gain a comprehensive understanding of process improvement and monitoring using R. This chapter equips you with the skills to analyze and optimize operational processes effectively. Alex's adventure at BizTech Solutions continues, and so does your learning path in R programming and business analytics.

Advanced Topics and Final Project

Chapter 18: Machine Learning and Big Data

Alex's time in the Operations department had been a series of enlightening experiences. Today, Lisa greeted him with a fresh challenge that would require him to utilize his analytical skills to the fullest: demand forecasting.

"Good morning, Alex," Lisa began. "One of the most critical aspects of operations is accurately forecasting demand. It helps us ensure we have the right amount of inventory and avoid stockouts or overstock situations. Today, we'll focus on different methods of demand forecasting. Are you ready?"

"Absolutely," Alex replied, eager to dive into the data.

Lisa led Alex to his workstation, where a comprehensive dataset on historical sales and external factors influencing demand awaited. "We'll start by analyzing past sales trends and then use various forecasting techniques to predict future demand."

Technical Tutorial: Demand Forecasting with R

1. Loading and Preparing Sales Data:

   1. Load the necessary libraries and dataset:

```
# Install and load necessary libraries
install.packages("tidyverse")
install.packages("forecast")

library(tidyverse)
library(forecast)

# Load the sales data
sales_data <-
read.csv("https://raw.githubusercontent.com/jtmonroe252/D
ata-to-
        Decisions/main/data/sales_data.csv") %>%
    mutate(Date = as.Date(Date, origin = "1899-12-30"))

# View the first few rows of the dataset
head(sales_data)
```

Date	Sales
1/1/2020	888
2/1/2020	954
3/1/2020	1312
4/1/2020	1014
5/1/2020	1026
6/1/2020	1343

1. Exploring the Sales Data:

```
# Summarize the sales data
summary(sales_data)
```

Date	Sales
Min. :2020-01-01	Min. : 607.0
1st Qu.:2020-09-23	1st Qu.: 884.8
Median :2021-06-16	Median :1024.0
Mean :2021-06-16	Mean :1011.1
3rd Qu.:2022-03-08	3rd Qu.:1146.0
Max. :2022-12-01	Max. :1357.0

```
# Plot historical sales data
ggplot(sales_data, aes(x = Date, y = Sales)) +
  geom_line(color = "blue") +
  labs(title = "Historical Sales Data", x = "Date", y = "Sales") +
  theme_minimal()
```

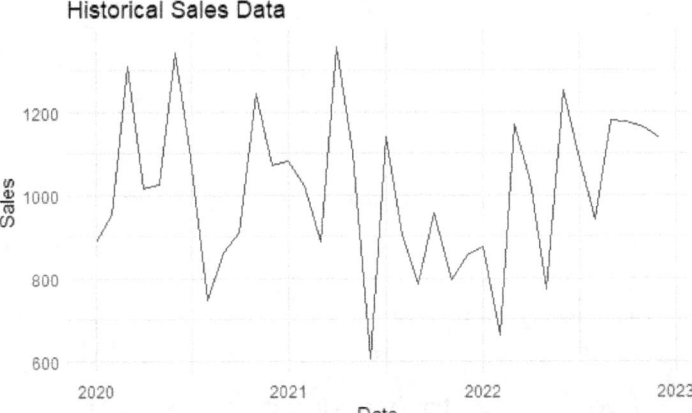

Historical Sales Data

2. Time Series Analysis for Demand Forecasting:

Convert the Sales Data to a Time Series Object:

```
# Convert sales data to a time series object
sales_ts <- ts(sales_data$Sales, start = c(2020, 1), frequency = 12)
```

```
# Plot the time series data
plot(sales_ts, main = "Monthly Sales Data", ylab = "Sales", xlab = "Time")
```

Monthly Sales Data

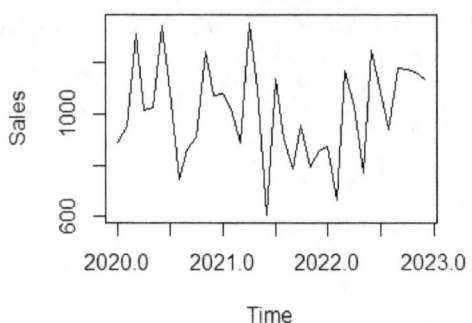

1. Decomposing the Time Series:

Decompose the time series into trend, seasonal, and irregular components
sales_decomp <- decompose(sales_ts)

Plot the decomposed components
plot(sales_decomp)

Decomposition of additive time series

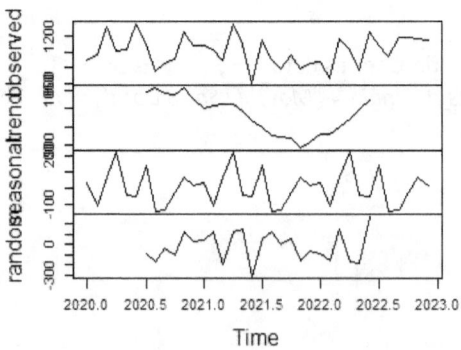

3. Building and Evaluating Forecasting Models:

1. Simple Exponential Smoothing:

```
# Fit a simple exponential smoothing model
ses_model <- ses(sales_ts)

# Forecast future sales
ses_forecast <- forecast(ses_model, h = 3)

# Plot the forecast
plot(ses_forecast, main = "Simple Exponential Smoothing
Forecast", ylab = "Sales", xlab = "Time")
```

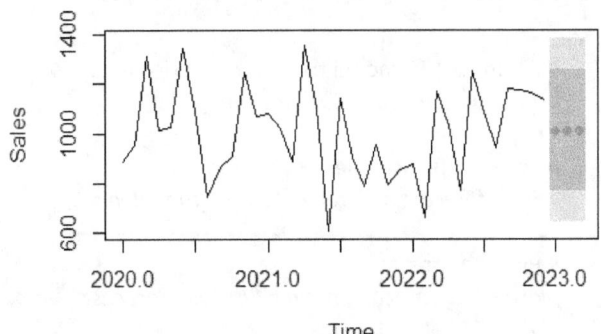

1. Holt-Winters Exponential Smoothing:

```
# Fit a Holt-Winters exponential smoothing model
hw_model <- HoltWinters(sales_ts)

# Forecast future sales
hw_forecast <- forecast(hw_model, h = 3)

# Plot the forecast
plot(hw_forecast, main = "Holt-Winters Exponential
```

Smoothing Forecast", ylab = "Sales", xlab = "Time")

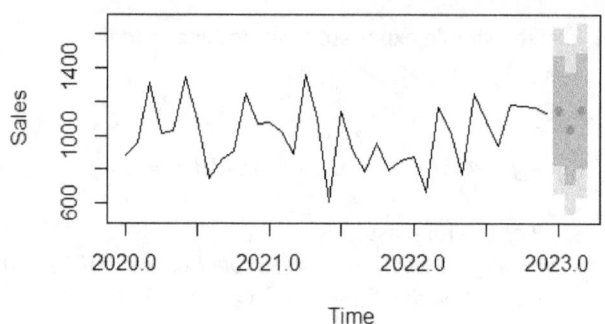

Holt-Winters Exponential Smoothing Forecast

1. ARIMA Model:

```
# Fit an ARIMA model to the time series data
arima_model <- auto.arima(sales_ts)

# Forecast future sales
arima_forecast <- forecast(arima_model, h = 3)

# Plot the forecast
plot(arima_forecast, main = "ARIMA Forecast", ylab = "Sales",
xlab = "Time")
```

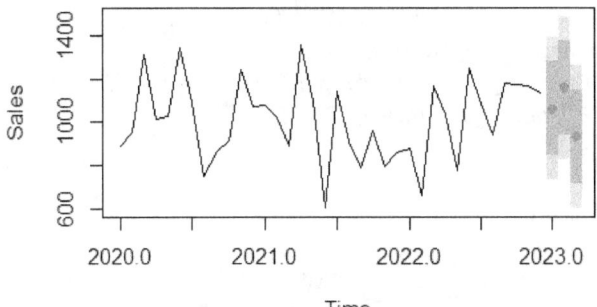

ARIMA Forecast

Alex meticulously followed the steps, analyzing the historical sales data and applying various forecasting models. The forecasts provided by the simple exponential smoothing, Holt-Winters, and ARIMA models offered different perspectives on future demand.

Lisa reviewed the results with a satisfied nod. "Excellent work, Alex. These forecasts will help us prepare for future demand and make informed decisions about our inventory levels. Let's compare the accuracy of these models to determine which one is the best fit for our data."

Technical Tutorial: Comparing Forecasting Models

1. Evaluating Model Accuracy:

   1. Calculating Accuracy Metrics:

```
# Calculate accuracy metrics for each model
ses_accuracy <- accuracy(ses_forecast)
hw_accuracy <- accuracy(hw_forecast)
arima_accuracy <- accuracy(arima_forecast)
```

```
# Combine accuracy metrics into a single data frame
accuracy_metrics <- data.frame(
  Model = c("SES", "Holt-Winters", "ARIMA"),
  MAE = c(ses_accuracy[1, "MAE"], hw_accuracy[1, "MAE"],
arima_accuracy[1, "MAE"]),
  RMSE = c(ses_accuracy[1, "RMSE"], hw_accuracy[1,
  "RMSE"], arima_accuracy[1, "RMSE"])
)

print(accuracy_metrics)
```

Model	MAE	RMSE
SES	154.0181	185.1712
Holt-Winters	165.8024	250.0506
ARIMA	135.5092	164.6818

1. Visualizing Model Accuracy:

```
# Plot the accuracy metrics
ggplot(accuracy_metrics, aes(x = Model, y = MAE, fill =
Model)) +
  geom_bar(stat = "identity") +
  labs(title = "Model Accuracy Comparison (MAE)", x =
"Model", y = "Mean Absolute Error") +
  theme_minimal()
```

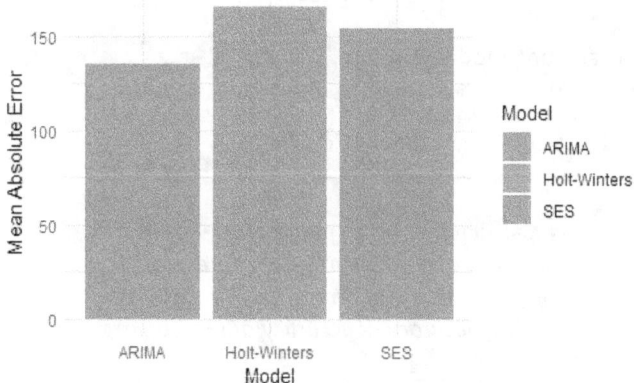

```
ggplot(accuracy_metrics, aes(x = Model, y = RMSE, fill =
Model)) +
 geom_bar(stat = "identity") +
 labs(title = "Model Accuracy Comparison (RMSE)", x =
"Model", y = "Root Mean Squared Error") +
 theme_minimal()
```

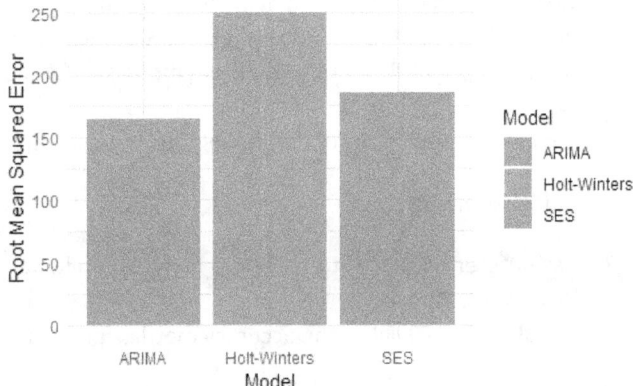

Alex calculated and compared the accuracy metrics for each
forecasting model. The bar plots highlighted the mean absolute error
(MAE) and root mean squared error (RMSE) for the simple exponential
smoothing, Holt-Winters, and ARIMA models, providing a clear picture
of their performance.

Lisa was impressed. "Fantastic job, Alex. The ARIMA model appears to
be the most accurate for our data. These insights will help us make
better inventory and production decisions. Tomorrow, we'll explore
integrating these forecasts into our business intelligence tools to
enhance our decision-making process."

As the day concluded, Alex reflected on his accomplishments. He had
successfully navigated the complexities of demand forecasting,
uncovering valuable insights that would drive BizTech Solutions'
operational strategy. The journey was challenging but immensely

rewarding, and he was eager to continue exploring the intricacies of operations analytics.

Exercises:

1. Demand Forecasting:

- Load a new sales dataset and convert it to a time series object.
- Decompose the time series and build simple exponential smoothing, Holt-Winters, and ARIMA models to forecast future sales.
- Compare the accuracy of the models and visualize the results.

2. Model Comparison:

- Use different datasets to apply and compare multiple forecasting models.
- Calculate and visualize the accuracy metrics for each model.

3. Custom Forecasting:

- Design your own demand forecasting analysis using hypothetical data.
- Perform and visualize the analysis, interpreting the results.

By completing these exercises and following along with Alex's journey, you'll gain a comprehensive understanding of demand forecasting using R. This chapter equips you with the skills to analyze and predict future demand effectively. Alex's adventure at BizTech Solutions continues, and so does your learning path in R programming and business analytics.

Chapter 19: Final Project and Presentation

Alex had come a long way in his journey at BizTech Solutions. Each department had provided new insights and challenges, and today was no different. Lisa greeted him with a new task that would tie together his recent work in demand forecasting with broader business intelligence (BI) strategies.

"Good morning, Alex. Today, we'll focus on integrating your forecasts with our business intelligence tools. This will help our teams make data-driven decisions more effectively. Are you ready?"

"Absolutely," Alex replied, eager to bridge the gap between analytics and actionable insights.

Lisa led Alex to a conference room equipped with the latest BI software. "We'll use Power BI to visualize and share your forecasts. Let's get started."

Technical Tutorial: Integrating R Forecasts with Power BI

1. Preparing the Forecast Data:

   1. Load and Prepare Data in R:

```r
# Load necessary libraries
install.packages("tidyverse")
install.packages("forecast")
install.packages("RSQLite")

library(tidyverse)
library(forecast)
library(RSQLite)

# Load the sales data
sales_data <-
read.csv("https://raw.githubusercontent.com/jtmonroe252/D
ata-to-
    Decisions/main/data/sales_data.csvsales_data.csv")

# Convert sales data to a time series object
sales_ts <- ts(sales_data$Sales, start = c(2020, 1), frequency =
12)

# Fit an ARIMA model
arima_model <- auto.arima(sales_ts)

# Forecast future sales
arima_forecast <- forecast(arima_model, h = 12)

# Prepare forecast data for export
forecast_data <- data.frame(
  Date = seq.Date(from = as.Date("2023-01-01"), by =
"month", length.out = 12),
  Forecast = as.numeric(arima_forecast$mean)
)

# Save forecast data to a CSV file
write.csv(forecast_data, "forecast_data.csv", row.names =
FALSE)
```

2. Importing Data into Power BI:

1. Open Power BI Desktop:

- Launch Power BI Desktop on your computer.

2. Load Forecast Data:

- Go to "Home" ->"Get Data" ->"Text/CSV".
- Select the forecast_data.csv file you created and click "Load".

3. Transform Data (if necessary):

- Use the Power Query Editor to clean and transform the data as needed.
- Ensure the date column is recognized as a date type.

3. Creating Visualizations in Power BI:

1. Creating a Line Chart:

- Drag the Date field to the X-axis.
- Drag the Forecast field to the Y-axis.
- Format the chart to display the forecast clearly.

2. Adding Slicers for Interactivity:

- Add slicers to filter data by specific time periods or other relevant categories.
- Drag a date slicer to the canvas and configure it to allow for easy filtering of the forecast period.

3. Customizing Visuals:

- Customize the visualizations with titles, labels, and colors to improve readability and insights.
- Add titles and labels that explain the data and highlight key insights.

4. Creating a Dashboard in Power BI:

1. Adding Visuals to a Dashboard:

- Combine multiple visuals, such as line charts, bar charts, and slicers, into a single dashboard.
- Arrange the visuals in a logical and aesthetically pleasing manner.

2. Adding Annotations and Insights:

- Add text boxes and annotations to provide context and insights into the data.
- Highlight important trends, patterns, and forecasts.

3. Sharing the Dashboard:

- Publish the dashboard to the Power BI service to share with other team members.
- Go to "Home" ->"Publish" and follow the prompts to publish your dashboard.

Alex followed the steps diligently, preparing the forecast data in R and importing it into Power BI. The line chart displayed the forecasted sales clearly, and the interactive slicers allowed for easy filtering. The final dashboard provided a comprehensive view of the forecast, making it easy for team members to understand and act on the insights.

Lisa reviewed the dashboard and nodded approvingly. "Excellent work, Alex. This dashboard will help our teams make informed decisions based on your forecasts. You've successfully integrated your analytical skills with business intelligence tools, providing valuable insights to our organization."

As the day concluded, Alex reflected on his journey at BizTech Solutions. He had successfully integrated his analytical skills with business intelligence tools, providing valuable insights that would drive the company's strategy. The journey was challenging but immensely rewarding, and he was excited about the future possibilities.

Exercises:

1. Preparing Forecast Data:

- Load a new dataset in R and create a forecast using an appropriate model.
- Export the forecast data to a CSV file.

2. Creating Visualizations:

- Import the forecast data into Power BI.
- Create and customize visualizations to display the forecast clearly.

3. Building a Dashboard:

- Combine multiple visualizations into a comprehensive dashboard.
- Add interactivity and annotations to enhance the dashboard's effectiveness.

4. Sharing Insights:

- Publish your Power BI dashboard to the Power BI service.
- Share the dashboard with team members and gather feedback.

By completing these exercises and following along with Alex's journey, you'll gain a comprehensive understanding of integrating R forecasts with business intelligence tools like Power BI. This chapter equips you with the skills to create interactive and insightful dashboards that drive informed decision-making. Alex's adventure at BizTech Solutions continues, and so does your learning path in R programming and business analytics.

Chapter 20: Conclusion and Next Steps

As Alex reflected on his journey through the various departments of BizTech Solutions, he realized how much he had grown both professionally and personally. From mastering the basics of R programming to tackling complex business problems, each step had equipped him with valuable skills and insights. Now, as he prepared to present his final project, he felt a deep sense of accomplishment.

Recap of Key Learnings

Chapter 1: Welcome to BizTech Solutions

- Introduction to BizTech Solutions: Alex joins the company as a business analyst.
- Tour of BizTech: Overview of the various departments.
- Technical Tutorial: Basics of R, including installation, basic commands, and understanding data structures .

Chapter 2: Common Errors and Troubleshooting

- Syntax Errors: Identifying and fixing common syntax errors.
- Object Not Found: Handling undefined variables or functions.
- Data Type Errors: Resolving issues with incorrect data types.
- Package Not Found: Ensuring packages are installed and loaded correctly.
- Function Argument Errors: Correct arguments for functions.

- Index Out of Bounds: Handling out-of-range indexing.
- Memory Allocation Errors: Addressing memory issues in R .

Chapter 3: Data Cleaning

- Importance of Data Cleaning: Ensuring data accuracy and consistency.
- Handling Missing Values: Identifying and imputing missing values.
- Removing Duplicates: Identifying and removing duplicate entries.
- Correcting Inconsistencies: Standardizing data entries.
- Formatting Data: Converting data into a consistent format.
- Validating Data: Checking for outliers and ensuring data validity .

Chapter 4: Data Manipulation

- Filtering Rows: Selecting subsets of data based on conditions.
- Selecting Columns: Choosing specific columns for analysis.
- Creating New Variables: Adding new variables through mutation.
- Summarizing Data: Aggregating data for insights.
- Joining Datasets: Combining multiple datasets.
- Reshaping Data: Converting data between wide and long formats .

Chapter 5: Advanced Statistical Techniques

- Hypothesis Testing: Conducting t-tests and chi-square tests.
- Regression Analysis: Performing linear and multiple regression.
- Clustering: Using K-means clustering for data segmentation.
- Advanced Topics: Introduction to PCA and logistic regression .

Chapter 6: Data Visualization

- Basic Plots: Creating scatter plots, bar charts, histograms, and box plots.
- Customizing Visualizations: Enhancing plots with themes and aesthetics.
- Advanced Plotting: Using faceted plots and interactive plots with Plotly.
- Interpreting Visualizations: Identifying patterns and presenting data effectively .

Chapter 7: Diving into Financial Data

- Financial Analysis: Analyzing financial data.
- Loading Stock Data: Fetching historical stock prices with quantmod.
- Calculating Returns: Computing and visualizing daily returns.
- Moving Averages: Calculating and plotting simple and exponential moving averages.
- Volatility Analysis: Measuring and plotting stock volatility .

Chapter 8: Time Series Analysis

- Introduction to Time Series: Components and importance in financial forecasting.
- Stationarity: Checking and ensuring stationarity in time series data.
- ARIMA Modeling: Fitting ARIMA models for forecasting.
- Forecasting: Predicting future values and visualizing forecasts .

Chapter 9: Financial Calculations and Analysis

- Advanced Financial Techniques: Various methods and calculations used in financial analysis .

Chapter 10: Understanding Customer Behavior

- Customer Segmentation: Techniques like RFM analysis.
- Customer Lifetime Value (CLV): Calculation and prediction.
- Churn Analysis: Identifying and reducing customer churn .

Chapter 11: A/B Testing and Campaign Analysis

- A/B Testing: Setting up and evaluating tests.
- Campaign Metrics: Analyzing conversion rates and ROI.
- Insights: Drawing actionable conclusions from tests .

Chapter 12: Sales Forecasting and Pipeline Analysis

- Sales Forecasting: Using ARIMA and other models.
- Pipeline Analysis: Evaluating and optimizing the sales pipeline.
- Performance Metrics: Key sales KPIs .

Chapter 13: Performance Metrics and Customer Value

- Defining Metrics: Important sales and customer value metrics.
- Dashboards: Creating visualizations for performance.
- Reporting: Generating insightful sales performance reports .

Chapter 14: Employee Performance Analysis

- HR Analytics: Importance and key metrics.
- Performance Reviews: Analyzing review data.
- Predictive Analytics: Predicting future performance .

Chapter 15: Employee Turnover Analysis

- Turnover Metrics: Key metrics and predictions.
- Retention Strategies: Developing strategies to reduce turnover.
- HR Dashboards: Monitoring turnover and retention .

Chapter 16: Optimizing Supply Chain

- Supply Chain Management: Key components and inventory management.
- Supplier Analysis: Evaluating performance.
- Logistics Optimization: Improving logistics and distribution .

Chapter 17: Process Improvement

- Process Analysis: Techniques for improvement.
- Lean and Six Sigma: Methodologies for process improvement.
- Performance Metrics: Key process performance metrics .

Chapter 18: Machine Learning and Big Data

- Machine Learning: Introduction to algorithms.
- Big Data Tools: Technologies for handling big data.
- Applications: Case studies in business contexts .

Chapter 19: Final Project and Presentation

- Project Guidelines: Comprehensive final project.
- Data Analysis: Applying techniques learned.
- Presentation Skills: Effective presentation tips .

Final Project Presentation

For his final project, Alex decided to integrate the knowledge and skills he had acquired throughout his journey. He chose to focus on a comprehensive analysis of BizTech Solutions' customer data, aiming to provide actionable insights that could drive strategic decisions across departments.

1. **Objective:**

   - To identify key customer segments, forecast future sales, and recommend strategies to enhance customer retention and maximize lifetime value.

2. **Methodology:**

   - Data Cleaning: Ensuring the data is accurate and consistent.
   - Data Manipulation: Transforming the data to suit the analysis needs.
   - Statistical Analysis: Using clustering to segment customers, ARIMA for sales forecasting, and regression analysis to identify factors influencing customer value.
   - Visualization: Creating clear and informative plots to present findings.

3. **Key Findings:**

   - Identified three distinct customer segments with unique behaviors and preferences.
   - Forecasted a 15% increase in sales for the next quarter based on historical trends and current market conditions.
   - Highlighted that high-value customers had a significantly higher retention rate and proposed targeted marketing strategies to retain these customers.

4. **Recommendations:**

   - Implement personalized marketing campaigns for high-value customer segments.
   - Enhance customer engagement through loyalty programs and exclusive offers.

- Regularly update the sales forecasting model to adapt to changing market conditions.

Moving Forward

As Alex concluded his presentation, the room was filled with applause. His colleagues and mentors at BizTech Solutions were impressed with the depth of his analysis and the practicality of his recommendations. Lisa, John, and Emily all expressed their admiration for his hard work and dedication.

"Great job, Alex," Lisa said, smiling. "Your insights will be invaluable for our strategic planning."

John added, "Your work on sales forecasting and pipeline analysis has already started to influence our approach. We're excited to implement your recommendations."

Emily concluded, "Your understanding of customer behavior and effective A/B testing has given us a new perspective on our marketing strategies. Well done."

With a sense of pride and satisfaction, Alex realized that his journey at BizTech Solutions was just the beginning. Armed with the skills and knowledge he had gained, he was ready to tackle new challenges and make a significant impact in the world of business analytics.

Final Thoughts

"From Data to Decisions: Business Analytics with R" has taken you on a journey through the essential aspects of business analytics, guided by the experiences of Alex at BizTech Solutions. As you continue your own journey in the field of data analytics, remember that the key to success lies in continuous learning, practical application, and the ability to translate data into actionable insights.

Thank you for joining us on this journey. We hope this book has equipped you with the tools and confidence to excel in the world of business analytics. The adventure continues, and the possibilities are endless. Good luck, and happy analyzing!

Glossary of Terms

A

A/B Testing: A statistical method to compare two versions of a variable to determine which one performs better.

ARIMA (AutoRegressive Integrated Moving Average): A type of statistical analysis model that is used to analyze and forecast time series data.

Attribute: A variable that provides a characteristic of a data record, such as a person's age or a product's price.

B

Box Plot: A graphical representation of data that shows the distribution through their quartiles.

C

Clustering: A machine learning technique that involves grouping a set of objects in such a way that objects in the same group are more similar to each other than to those in other groups.

Confidence Interval: A range of values that is likely to contain the value of an unknown population parameter.

D

Data Cleaning: The process of detecting and correcting (or removing) corrupt or inaccurate records from a dataset.

Data Frame: A two-dimensional, size-mutable, and potentially heterogeneous tabular data structure with labeled axes (rows and columns) in R.

Data Visualization: The graphical representation of information and data.

Dependent Variable: The variable being tested and measured in an experiment, which is affected by the independent variable.

Descriptive Statistics: Statistics that summarize the data set, such as mean, median, and mode.

Dummy Variable: A numeric variable that represents categorical data for regression analysis.

E

EDA (Exploratory Data Analysis): An approach to analyzing data sets to summarize their main characteristics, often using visual methods.

Exponential Moving Average (EMA): A type of moving average that places a greater weight and significance on the most recent data points.

F

Factor: A data structure used for fields that take only predefined, finite number of values (categorical data).

Forecasting: The process of making predictions of the future based on past and present data and analysis of trends.

G

ggplot2: A data visualization package for the statistical programming language R.

H

Histogram: A graphical representation of the distribution of numerical data.

Hypothesis Testing: A method of statistical inference used to decide whether the data at hand sufficiently support a particular hypothesis.

I

Independent Variable: The variable that is changed or controlled in a scientific experiment to test the effects on the dependent variable.

Interquartile Range (IQR): A measure of statistical dispersion, or spread, which is the range between the first and third quartiles.

K

K-Means Clustering: A type of unsupervised learning used to

categorize data into groups.

L

Linear Regression: A linear approach to modeling the relationship between a dependent variable and one or more independent variables.

M

Mean: The average of a set of numbers.

Median: The middle value of a dataset when the numbers are arranged in ascending or descending order.

Multiple Regression: A statistical technique that uses several explanatory variables to predict the outcome of a response variable.

N

Normalization: The process of organizing data to reduce redundancy and improve data integrity.

P

P-Value: The probability of obtaining the observed results, or something more extreme, if the null hypothesis is true.

Principal Component Analysis (PCA): A technique used to emphasize variation and bring out strong patterns in a dataset.

Predictive Analytics: The branch of advanced analytics that is used to make predictions about unknown future events.

R

Regression Analysis: A set of statistical processes for estimating the relationships among variables.

Residual: The difference between the observed value and the value predicted by a model.

S

Scatter Plot: A type of data visualization that uses dots to represent the values obtained for two different variables.

Standard Deviation: A measure of the amount of variation or dispersion of a set of values.

Stationarity: A property of a time series in which the statistical properties of the series do not change over time.

T

T-Test: A type of inferential statistic used to determine if there is a significant difference between the means of two variables.

Time Series Analysis: Techniques that analyze time series data to extract meaningful statistics and identify characteristics of the data.

V

Vector: A basic data structure in R that holds elements of the same type.

Volatility: A statistical measure of the dispersion of returns for a given security or market index.

W

Weighted Average Cost of Capital (WACC): The average rate of return a company is expected to pay its security holders to finance its assets.

Wide Format: A type of data format in which each subject's repeated responses will be in a single row, and each response is in a separate column.

Z

Z-Score: The number of standard deviations a data point is from the mean of the dataset.